Going Deeper In

John "Geordie" Gordon

ISBN 978-1-78222-834-9

Front cover photo: Pixabay

Book design, layout and production management by Into Print www.intoprint.net

+44 (0)1604 832149

THE START OF IT ALL

The train journey home gave me time to think. Although my face was a mess and everyone on the train was staring, probably wondering how the hell I'd got into that state, at a football game, fighting the other team's supporters or a car crash. What they thought I wasn't concerned about, but how my Mam would react seeing me in this state, that was my worry. My face was still black and blue, stitches in my left eye and my top lip. My dad would be hoping it was in a fight, and that I had won (to be fair it was, but not the sort he would have hoped). My head was in a spin; who had put that letter in the envelope? How did it get into camp? And who was sick enough to do such a thing after what I had just been through? I couldn't get my head around it. I was starting to sweat, my back was sticking to the seat I had claimed by the window in the second carriage. No one could get in the SAS camp without a pass, and it was well guarded. It *had* to be someone inside – but *who*? That I couldn't answer. I took my bag off the seat at the side of me. I reached in and pulled out my first can of lager for what seemed like weeks. I started flicking the top of the can, for what reason I didn't know, it was something I had picked up from the lads. I pulled the ring and heard that sweet sound. I started to drink and the gold liquid flowed down my throat with the sound of a stream rippling over the pebbles in the morning sunlight. It felt good and immediately my head started to clear. I forgot about the note in my pocket.

I sat drinking the lager, looking out the window. I thought of what I had been through over the last week and a half, and asked myself if I fancied going through it again. Then it hit me – what I had been through wouldn't happen again if I became one of the team. I had been one of the hunted, and not the hunter. I had to think differently to the approach. If I could help stop this happening to just one unfortunate young lad, I would be doing something good. After the bullying I had gone through at school and what I had just been through, I felt my life had been turned around; I had learned to stand up for myself and my friends, and even when I was getting a good kicking, I took it and didn't back down or run from it. I stood and took the lot. Above all, I could take it and come out the other side still standing tall; I had been accepted into the army, the lads hadn't judged me, tested me yes, but I came through that as well, and had become part of something big, a *family*. This was not the same as your family with Mam, Dad, brother and sisters, but something just as strong – or perhaps something even stronger.

My family at home was always strong, not just brother and sisters, but in-laws too. One of my brothers-in-law, John Alexander, was married to my oldest sister Anne. He seemed to look after me, for what reason I didn't know. He would take me out for a drive in his car, invite me to the club with his mates, and he and my sister Anne would have parties at their home, and invite me to them as well. I feel I owe him so much; he made me feel just like all the other lads, part of something, I had a place in life, and I thank him and my sister Anne for that.

I now knew I had to go for the team and hoped everyone else did as well. I sank about six cans. I hadn't spoken to or even looked at anyone for the whole journey up to that point. The train stopped at Doncaster and people got on and off. The seat opposite had been empty for the whole journey but then a middle-aged lady boarded and asked if the seat was taken. No, fill your boots I said, and continued looking out of the window with my can for comfort.

She was struggling to put her bag in the overhead rack, so I put my can down and grabbed her bag. I hadn't even asked her if she needed help. I thought what a shit, neither she nor any of the other people on the train had done a thing to me, and I had no reason to be a twat to them. As I was putting her bag away she thanked me and then sat opposite on the other side of the table. "You been in a fight son?" That was the first time anyone on the train had asked, although they'd all kept looking, none had had the balls to ask.

"Yes, something like that," I said. I picked up my can and started drinking again. The lady had a bag on the seat next to her, she put it on her knees and opened it, took out a lunch box and offered me a sandwich. I was feeling a bit peckish but refused and thanked her.

"Would you like a can?" I picked one up and held it in front of her. "Yes, I don't mind if I do," she said, as she took it out of my hand. I was thinking she seemed to be an alright lady. "You travelling far?" I asked. "Just up to Newcastle, you?" "Yes, the same."

We got chatting. She told me about her job, travelling up and down the country putting large companies' finances right. She had to be very clever, but yet she seemed down to earth, sitting on a train drinking a can of lager and eating a sandwich. "What is it you do?" she asked. "Am in the army, just going home for a couple of weeks leave," I replied. "I like a man in uniform," she said with a smile on her face. The conversation flowed and we seemed to get on OK. Just as the train was pulling into Newcastle station, she asked if I fancied a drink in one of the pubs over the road from the station. Why not? I thought. She seemed OK and there was no harm in it.

We had to have been chatting for about three hours, and for some strange reason I wanted to tell her all about my ordeal out on the Yorkshire moors. However, I held off. She asked if I fancied meeting up for a drink one day while I was on leave. She gave me a phone number that she had scribbled down on a beer mat. "Ring me if you fancy it," she said. She stood up and kissed me on the lips and smiled. "You're a good-looking lad underneath that bruising." I had forgotten about it, I just seemed to be fixed on her. At that she walked to the door, stopped, turned back, gave a cheeky smile and left.

I sat and finished my drink. What does she want with me? I thought. After I'd finished my pint, I had a quick look at my watch and decided not to go home that night. I'd stay and have a few more drinks before booking into the station hotel that was just over the road from the pub. I could handle all the questions about the state of my face and how I got it. Once again I noticed people looking at me, but by now I couldn't give a hoot, I just sat looking absently through the window opposite. Next thing I knew, the barman was calling last orders. I walked to the bar to have a last drink. Once I had been served, I stood at the end of the bar with my drink. After I'd drained the last mouthful, I put the empty glass down on the counter before walking out of the bar and across to the hotel.

The town seemed quiet, not a lot of people around for the time of year. Once I'd booked in for the night, I headed straight to the room, dropped my bags on the floor and lay down on top of the bed. I must have fallen asleep instantly, as the next thing I knew it was morning and I was still fully dressed. I got up and looked out of the window. The sky was blue, the sun shining, and I felt a lot better. I stripped off, dropped my clothes on the floor and went into the shower.

It felt good. I put my hands on the tiled wall, tilted my head back and let the water hit my face. I knew that I was feeling better, as the warm water on my face felt great and there was no pain. Once I had finished and got myself dressed, I headed down for breakfast, a full English, just what I needed. I was now feeling a lot better in myself and ready to head home.

When I checked out the young lady behind the reception desk asked if I had enjoyed my stay. Yes, fine thank you, and I may call again soon. I was thinking of the lady I had spent the night drinking with, hoping one day I might call her. I headed out for the bus home, but I felt I should phone my Mam first, just to give her the heads up on my face situation.

Mam was a great lady, I know everyone says that about their Mam, but she was extra special. When she was about 14 years old, she lost her own Mam at the age of thirty-four, so she had to step up to be Mam to her younger brother and sisters, then she lost her dad only a few years later, so she then had the whole family to look after. She then went on to have nine children of her own. She gave us all she could, and we may not have had a lot, but we all had love. It was important to contact her, because I knew she would have a fit if I didn't warn her.

She was so glad to hear my voice and to know I was home. "I will have your favourite waiting for you when you get in," she said. It was always the same, ham and pease pudding stottie, the best welcome home a Geordie could ask for.

As I got off the bus, I could see her and two of my sisters looking out of the living room window, the smiles on their faces said it all. The front door opened as I approached it, my Mam stood with her arms outstretched, the look on her face was a sight to behold, she seemed to have all emotions in her eyes, happy I was back, sad I looked a mess, and proud I was in the army. I hugged her and suddenly I felt safe. A tear ran down my cheek, and as two of my sisters hugged around the two of us, I felt relief, from what I didn't know, but I also felt proud. I had come through and survived everything that had happened in the short time I had been in the army.

Going back to camp was the one thing I couldn't wait for, but it was pointless at the moment even thinking about it as the camp would be in lockdown for the next two weeks. I was also thinking whether I should go for the team or not. But if I did, this time I would be with Tony and the lads, and would have a proper chance to show off the other side of my military skills. Before I could do that, however, I had to get through my time at home with my family and friends.

I sat on Dad's chair next to the window and had my sandwich and cuppa. We chatted for a while, about nothing much, I think they were a bit scared, not knowing what I had been through and the state of my face put them off a bit. I asked Mam if Dad was at work. "No he is at the club, why don't you go up and have a drink with him?"

"I think I will," I replied.

I finished my sandwich and cuppa, gave Mam a kiss and headed to the club. As I walked up the street, I was thinking of what I would tell him about my face – the truth or should I make up a story? I couldn't lie to him, he could always tell when I was lying. I knew I wasn't to speak about what had happened but *how could I get out of it?* As I walked up to the club, I was still thinking what to say, when I heard a voice from the other side of the street; it was a voice I would never forget, Dave McGlen, my best mate. It was great to see him again. We shook hands, and he started asking about the army. "You still getting a good kicking?" he queried when he saw my face. "No mate," I said casually, "I won this one." That wasn't a lie, and that's what I would tell Dad. I couldn't come up with anything else. It wouldn't make me look as if I had lied, I hadn't, I just hadn't told the full truth.

We walked into the club and saw Dad sitting in his usual seat with his best mate Geordie Hall. They were more like brothers than mates, they did everything together, or at least that's what it seemed like. We always called him Uncle Geordie, and to me that's what he always would be. Their normal drinking place was The Norwood; why they had changed I didn't know. Sat next to them I noticed Freddy Bamburgh, he was the man that had helped me with the training to join the army in the first place, he was also an ex SAS soldier. I could speak to him. I felt relief thinking I could speak about what had happened to me, Brit and Kenny. Nonetheless, I had a nervous feeling in my stomach and I didn't know if it was because I felt I could speak about it, or simply that I was nervous about speaking to *him*, in case he went off it that I had broken the code of the army. When they say don't speak about something, you don't.

My dad got out of his seat, put his hand out to me. We shook hands and as I'd thought, asked if I had won the fight. As I grabbed his hand, I replied if I hadn't I wouldn't be there. For the first time ever, he told me to sit down while he got me a pint. In the past he would have just handed me the money and told me to get the drinks. I sat next to Freddy and I told Dave to sit opposite. "No mate, I'll let you catch up with your dad, I'll have a pint with my dad, and I'll see you later." He pointed across the room to indicate where he was going to sit. I looked over and saw his dad was having a game of cards with his mate. Just at that moment he looked up and gave me a wave and a small smile with a wink, as if to say he was proud and glad to see me home with my best mate. Dave smiled and left me to chat with my dad and his mates. Dad came back from the bar with the drinks, put them on the table in front of me and looked at me without saying a word. That was the first time I had read his face without being scared, normally the look from him was a telling off, or get ready for a hiding. We chatted for about thirty minutes before I got up for the toilet.

As I was standing at the urinal, Freddy walked in. He waited until the two other men there had left, and then, looking at the wall in front of him, said:

"Do we need to speak in private?"

I looked down at the floor.

John William Gordon

"Geordie"

Army Service 1977 to 1993
Royal Regiment Fusiliers 1977 to 1980
Royal Artillery 1980 to 1993

I was nervous. I couldn't look at him but I had to speak, if I could. Again, no eye contact, just: "Come to my house at 16:00 hours today ... and don't tell anyone you're coming." He finished and left, and I was left standing thinking if I had done the right thing or not. Would he be upset with me for speaking about it or glad I had spoken to him and no one else? I would just have to wait and see, it was too late now to change my mind. I headed back to the bar.

My dad's best mate, Geordie Hall, was just like Dad, a jack the lad. They would do anything to make a bob or two – straight or not. Although at Christmas they would raise money to get toys for all the kids in hospital, and organise a party for the pensioners on the estate. I remember one time, Dad took me and my brother to the allotment to dig it over for him. This was not unusual as Michael my brother, Bobby and Keith (Geordie's sons) all used to have jobs to do in the allotment. But one day Dad gave me and Micky (that's what we all called Michael) a bucket each to get coal from outside the fence at the coke works. We decided to go and play for a while, down on the site where the A1 western bypass was being built. While we were messing around I noticed a coal seam in the wall of one of the deep holes there, so we filled the buckets with it so we could play a bit longer. When we got back to the allotment we gave Dad the buckets. He looked at them and asked where we had got the coal from. Micky straight away said outside the fence.

Mark Britnel

"Brit"

Royal Artillery, 1979 to 2005

"Don't you try that one, the size of this lot couldn't fall through the fence!" We both looked at the buckets, then each other. Dad was right, some of the coal bits had to be about the size of building bricks. We had to tell him and then he marched us down to where we had got it. Little did we know, it was a massive seam. Dad left us there and headed off for Geordie and his two lads … and about 40 sacks! We had to fill them every day for the six weeks of school holidays. Dad and Geordie would load the van and take them around the doors for the old people, as there was a strike on for the miners. He'd give them free, but sell any they had left. We never saw a penny, well, me and Micky never did, but Keith and Bobby did, as they lived on the side of the estate where the coal was. They would hide two or three bags and then sell them themselves – again, we didn't get a share. It's quite strange as we are all so much like our dads: we will do anything to make a bob or two, but still help anyone that needs it, and even now I still consider them as family.

Geordie just came out with it. "Was that the Argentinians that done that son?" My dad piped up, "Never mind, he'll tell us when he's ready." I just said no, it was a couple of dicks at camp, and it ended there, I went off and had a game of pool with one of my mates. He asked the same question, but I stuck to the story. When the club called last orders, we finished our drinks and left. Me and Dad left his mate on the corner of Rothberry Gardens and headed home. We chatted about nothing, until he asked again about my face. "Can I just leave it for now Dad?" I said. "No problem son, I'm here if you need to speak." Dad had been in the army himself, so I think he knew if you had been in a conflict with the army, some people didn't want to speak about it at first, but as time went on you would open up and speak to someone one day, and dad was hoping it would be him. I also hoped it would be him, but because of what I had gone through, I didn't want Dad to worry.

Kenny had spent another three days in hospital, but as soon as he was discharged he headed home to Hartlepool. Back home, Kenny didn't have any problem with questions; he was always in fights, so no one asked, just *did you win?* He was the same as me, having trouble with himself and questioning constantly. How did we get into this mess? and could we handle the team? Brit, however, had no trouble with any of it, he just wanted revenge, and he had to work on Dunc, because he wasn't up for it when we left Hereford. He was having one week with his family and then heading to London to spend the second week with Brit.

Me and Dad got home and sat down to dinner. Mam always had Dad his dinner on the table for him as he walked through the door. After dinner Dad headed off to bed as he always did after a drink; it was now 15:30 hours and I had to head off to see Freddy. I told Mam I was going to see my best mate Dave McGlen — I wasn't and felt horrible fibbing to Mam and the rest of them but I had to do it.

As I walked along the street I started getting a horrible feeling in my stomach, my hands started shaking, I didn't know if I was scared of Freddy or of what I was going to say to him. As I approached his house I felt myself slowing down, trying to give myself more time, but it didn't matter how slow I went I knew I had to speak to him, just to see if I was right to go for the team.

I stood at Freddy's door and took a deep breath before I

knocked and waited; I could feel the sweat running down my neck, my palms were itching. The door opened and Freddy filled it with his big frame. "Come in son," he said as he stepped to one side. I took two steps into the hallway. "Go through," he said as he pointed to the living room. I walked in as he shut the front door. I stood to one side as he came though. "Sit down, I'm not going to bite you. Well, the house is empty and we aren't going to be interrupted," he assured me, "so start at the beginning ... and I know all of *this*," pointing at my face, "wasn't done in the Falklands."

"I'm sorry I have been told not to speak about it to anyone."

"I'm not anyone," he said a little impatiently. "You know what I was, so start, get on with it."

I knew I couldn't back out now so I began. I started from going to the club, giving him the lot up to getting on the train home.

"One thing I will tell you," he said, "*everyone* has to speak to someone about things like this. I did when I was involved in some really dangerous tasks, but one thing you must remember is they *have* to be trusted. You need to speak about anything you speak to *me*, not your dad or Dave your mate, as for what you should do, how long is your leave for?"

Two weeks I told him.

"Then stay at home for a week, get some training done, and sharpen your reflexes up, you'll need them when you go back to the group."

That seemed to be the answer, I was going to the group, whether I was up for it or not. Freddy continued, "You need to focus on training, You get someone to train with you, and make sure they're fit and up for it."

Dave McGlen was the one I thought of straight away, he was fit. Every time we trained we would push each other to the limit, always trying to beat each other. If we started with the karate, we would have Chris McKenner pushing us. Chris was my instructor before I joined the army, he trained us hard and was good at it; at the time he was a Third Dan black belt. This I had to do.

After the chat Freddy sent me off home and I was to report to him every second day. He would just check how I was doing and if I felt up to the group.

Each day I felt more and more up for it. The training got harder and harder as the days went on, Dave would push me and Chris wouldn't let us stop; training with the two of them made it hard but worth it. At nights I would go off on my own, stick a 30lb pack on my back and head off for a five or six mile run. I would head off along the coach road, an old country lane and then up Silver Hills. The route was about three miles long and very steep; it was hard but I would push myself all the way to the top. At times I would be crying with the pain, but just like we would say, *no pain no gain*. Once I hit the top a force march would come into action for the rest of the way home. Some of the lads thought I was mad but I felt it had to be done. Dave came with me one night; he didn't have the pack on his back but still struggled to keep with me. It felt good, Dave was one of the fittest lads I knew, to see him struggle with the run made me see I was getting somewhere. I continued with the training for the next week and Chris and Dave pushed me every day. I also continued to visit Freddy, and what he did for me was magic, the things he spoke about I would never repeat, but he got through to me in a way you would never believe.

Each night after I had my run I would head for the club
and have a pint or two with my dad or my mates. Me and
Dad didn't see eye to eye before I joined up, but this week
was different, we hit it off brilliantly. He was a hard man and
didn't back down to anyone, if you did wrong you would
know all about it. I remember one night when I was a kid I
had to take the dogs for a walk – I had whippets and used to
race them. I would take them for walks for about 5 miles. On
this particular night there was a disco on at the youth club,
so I had them out for about ten minutes, enough time for
them to do their business, took them home and headed off
to the club. When Dad got home he asked if the dogs had
been out. Mam dropped me in it. Not thinking she said "for
about ten minutes". Dad got in his car and headed for the
youth club. He walked through the doorway and called out
my name, *JOHN*. He was so loud everyone stopped what
they were doing, I even think the record stopped. He kicked
me from the door of the club right to the car, drove me
home without saying a word. I didn't have a clue what I had
done wrong, but I wasn't going to ask. When we got home
he booted me into the house. "YOU WANT TO RACE THE DOGS
THEN YOU TRAIN THEM, NOW GET THEM OUT FOR A WALK!" I
didn't say a word, I just got the dogs and off I went. As I
walked them, I was thinking big, I was about 14 at the time,
and was thinking I could take him, so I decided to keep the
dogs out until late. For the whole of the walk I just kept on
thinking I would take him – I did live in dreamland, there
was no way I could, but stupid me thought different – why,
I didn't have a clue. I couldn't even stand up for myself at
school never mind against my dad. When I entered the street
at about ten minutes after midnight, my dad's van wasn't at

the door. Great, I thought, all that big talk I had given myself I was starting to think in real life he would kill me. I started to hurry up the street, just to get in before him. When I knocked on the door, I had the dogs off the leads. The door opened, the dogs ran in and my Mam stood crying.

"Where do you think you've been, your dad is out looking for you?"

I could feel the blood drain from my body, my hands started to sweat, and my face must have turned white as the blood had gone. If I can get to bed before he came in, I might get away with it until the morning at least, I thought. Not a chance. I was just about to put my left foot in the doorway, when I heard the voice that always sent a shiver down my spine, *DON'T YOU GO IN THAT HOUSE*. Dad was coming down the street in his van. Mam went into the living room to get away from it, she hated Dad hitting us.

As Dad got out of the van for some reason I had the feeling I could take him on. I had two dog leads in my hand; one I wrapped around my hand, the other I held tight ready to swing at him. As he walked towards me, he stared at me. *"WHERE THE HELL DO YOU THINK YOU'VE BEEN?"* Stupid me replied "for a walk". I just got the words out of my mouth and *bang!* His fist landed right on the end of my nose. I felt it crack as I fell back against the trellis.

He threw me into the garden and continued to lay the punches to my face. I felt I was going to die and tried desperately to shield my face, but his fist just kept finding gaps. I'd never had a kicking like it, and after he finished Dad just walked back into the house. I didn't know if I should run or go in and probably get another kicking. As I struggled to my feet, Mam was at the door, tears running down her cheeks. "Get in and go straight to bed." Blood was all over my face. When I was in the hallway, Dad called out, "Get in here!" Mam wouldn't dare go against Dad, but she whispered "don't say anything" as I headed in, my tail between my legs. All the while I was shaking and wishing I had never gone for that walk, wishing I hadn't thought I was big, wishing I was back in the school yard getting a kicking from the lads – it would be easier and probably not as painful. When I opened the living room door, Dad was sat in his chair, his face said it all; he was angry and upset that I had even thought of having a go. I didn't try that again for a long time.

I was glad I had come home when I did. Me and Dad had a bit of time together having a pint. Walking up and down to the club we would chat about times at the caravan up at Amble, where he would get me and my brother Micky to meet him at the Scooner pub. The fishermen would have a box of crabs for us to sell around the caravan site, 25p each, but we would sell them for 50p and keep half of the money. He would laugh and tell me about things he got up to as a kid, like the time he got into trouble from his mam for taking a horse upstairs into his bedroom.

Time was getting on; I only had five days left before I had to head back to camp, so I thought about the last time I'd visited Freddy – it was about 19:00 hours on a Wednesday night. He'd sat me down in his living room, and began to go through things we had spoken about over the last week or so. "Now it's time for you to leave and get away from here. You don't tell *anyone* you're leaving, you need to just pack a bag and go, stay somewhere where you can get your family out of your head. To do what you're going back to, your family has to be well gone, or you will never get through it."

At the time I didn't understand what he meant, but as time went on I started to get it. When you're on a mission the last people you need in your head is family, you can't focus and a discussion about family can cost you your life, but far worse is it can cost the life of one of your mates.

As I walked home from Freddie's that night, I couldn't stop thinking he was right, I was feeling bad I wouldn't be saying goodbye to Mam and sisters. My brother was different, he didn't care, or that's what he would portray, but underneath I knew he missed me when I was away with the army. Would Dave understand or would he think I was ungrateful for all the help he and Chris had given me? No matter what I had to leave; I had to go somewhere where I was unknown.

Freddy advised me to book into a B&B "… and you will work it out yourself what to do. If you stay, you'll end up speaking about it to someone, so it's best you go. I will tell you this, whatever you decide it has to be *your* decision. I'll speak to your dad tomorrow, so don't worry about your family." We spoke about things he had been through with the SAS, and how it had made him what he is today. I had a good feeling about myself. I got up and thanked him, and headed home.

That night when I went to bed, I packed my bag and pushed it under the bed. I lay on top of the bed and just stared at the ceiling until about 02:30, trying to think of a place to go. Later, when I got up to leave the house, I had to be so quiet as Micky was on the bottom bunk. I grabbed my cash off the windowsill and noticed among it a folded piece of paper. I opened it out and recognised the phone number from the lady off the train. *That was it*, I would call her in the morning, and until then I would stay at the station hotel in the town centre. The name next to the number was Paula. That was the first time I'd thought of her since she'd left the pub after we had that drink. I crept down the stairs slowly to make no noise, and after closing the door quietly behind me, I set off down the street. Once I got to the corner, I stopped and looked back. I wished I didn't have to do this, but I knew I had to sort my head out; I had to decide if this was for me, or did I just want to be a run of the mill soldier. This would probably be one of the biggest decisions I would make in my life, because I knew it was going to be hard mentally and physically, but more than that it would be dangerous – a life and death situation.

By this time Kenny was on the mend and back in Hartlepool at his dad's. He didn't need to think what to do, his main reason for joining the army was to join the SAS, and this would be a great start to gain experience. During his time at home, all he did was train. He would go to the boxing club twice a day and work himself into the ground. Glenn was much the same as Kenny. Before Glenn left the camp to head home, he had popped to the hospital to see Kenny; they had agreed to only spend one week at the most at home, meet up in the Hull area, and do the last week living off the land, practising their survival skills deep in a forest. Tony spent his time at home with his brothers; he had decided what he was doing and felt he didn't need the extra training; he was one of the fittest in the regiment, he could catch up with any training that may be needed. Jock and Platty had spent the two weeks in Burnley at Platty's mam's house; they too had decided what they were doing, and had started preparing themselves for the next task. Donny had to think about what he was going to do as he was planning to get married and was wondering what impact it would have on his marriage; his wife to be wasn't from a military background, so she would find it hard to adjust being away from home, her family and friends. Dunc was the one we all had concerns about. Brit had taken him to London to stay with him and his Mam.

They knocked on the door. His mam opened it and looked at them. Brit's face was still a mess, but the response from his mam was, *you still bloody fighting, I thought you would've settled with the army.* She stepped forward to him, put her arms out and hugged him. "This is my mate Dunc," he said. She turned and looked at him. "You a friend of his?" she asked., "Yes? Then you're welcome." She hugged him and said, "Make yourself at home son, I'll put the kettle on."

Dunc could handle himself but wasn't into this kind of stuff, Brit had his work cut out trying to convince him to go with the team, but to be fair he had seen a lot of horror in his time in the army. As luck would have it, Brit took Dunc out for a drink to his local on the Old Kent Road. They met up with Brit's old mates and had a good time. The drink was flowing and all were having a good night. At the end of the night, they headed home, calling to the chippy on the way. As they were walking they noticed a club on the opposite side of the street. They could hear an argument between some lads, but decided to keep out of it and continued walking until a scream of a young girl rang out. They both stopped and looked back.

There was one young lad on the ground and three doormen laying into him. Dunc dropped his chips and ran over to help him, Brit had no choice but to follow. As they approached the group the doormen stepped back. Dunc grabbed the young lad, he was out of it, the young girl was sobbing and shouting at the doormen calling them bullies. When Brit joined him they picked the lad up and helped him away. He soon came around, and was unaware of what had happened. Brit asked the girl what had happened.

"We had been in the club and some lads had been messing about, one of them thought it would be funny to grab my tits, I hit him in the face, so he set about my boyfriend, the doormen came and grabbed my boyfriend, and dragged him outside, I was trying to tell them it wasn't him that started it, but they didn't care, and that's when they bashed him."

Dunc flagged down a taxi for them, got the young lad in and gave the driver a couple of quid and asked him to take them home. Dunc was fuming about what had happened, and wanted to go to the club and have it out with them. However, Brit stopped him. "It isn't worth it mate, that's why we have to be part of the group, to stop this sort of thing happening. Count me in, we'll put a stop to this, if it's the last thing I do."

Brit was over the moon, he thought Dunc was the only one they needed to convince to stay with the group, little did he know BSM Bob was out.

Bob had a family and was happy to stay in the army, but this type of thing was not for him at this time of his army life. He and his wife had settled. After the number of conflicts he had been involved in, he thought it was time to concentrate on his family.

Glenn Harwood

Falklands 1982
12 Air Defence Regiment, Royal Artillery
Main Weapon, Rapier

I turned and headed along Beechwood Gardens, thinking should I walk to the town or call a taxi. When I got to the phone box, I opened the door and looked in. The decision had been made for me – the receiver had been smashed – so I had to walk.

When I got to the hotel I went to the bar and had a couple of pints before I headed to the room. I stripped and climbed into bed. I was ready for a good sleep and didn't wake until 11:30 the next day.

I showered, got dressed, headed down for breakfast, but of course I was too late, breakfast had finished at 10:00 hours, so

I decided to check out and then made my way over the road to a café, where I got myself a full English and a pot of tea.

I sat by a window sipping the tea and looking at the phone number I had been given off Paula, wondering if I should phone. The waitress brought my food, I thanked her and put the scrap of paper back in my pocket. Once I had finished the late breakfast, I sat for a while just enjoying the morning sun coming over the top of the station hotel and shining through the window onto my face; it was good to feel it without pain in my eyes. My face was starting to heal, the bruising was fading and I was starting to look normal at last. I decided to phone her. As I walked over to the station to find a working phone box, I kept changing my mind. Would I head back to camp or not? Finally I found a phone box. I took the crumpled piece of paper with Paula's number and dialled. I had three 10p coins ready to feed it. The phone rang about five times before the pips started to go. I pushed in the first 10p, waited for the connection … "Hello, is that Paula?" I said.

Silence. Not a sound from the other end for about 3 seconds, no *who is this?* Then came a man's voice on the other end. "I'm John, is Paula there?" I began to think she was married. No voice came back for a further few seconds, then, "Yes, wait a minute, I'll fetch her." I waited a short while, then a voice from the other end, "Hi, can I help you?"

"Yes, it's John from the train journey, you gave me your number."

"Oh yes, how're you doing?"

"OK, but I was hoping we could meet up."

"Not a problem."

"Who was that man that answered the phone?"

"That's my house mate, we share to keep the bills down. Do you know Jesmond?" she asked.

"Yes, a little."

"Do you know the health centre? … Yes? There's a pub next to it, The Dog and Duck, do you want to meet me there at 3?"

"Yes, that's fine, see you then," I said, and put the receiver back down on its holder, checking my watch as I pushed the door open. I had about two and a half hours to kill before I would make my way to meet her, but I didn't want to walk around town in case I bumped into someone I knew, so I headed off to the bus station and jumped on a bus to Jesmond.

The bus dropped me outside a row of shops and pubs. I had a pint in one of the pubs at the bottom of the estate while I waited for her. The time was now 14:00 hours so I headed to the pub where we'd agreed to meet. I walked in and had a good look around. I noticed a table in the corner that would give me all round vision of the pub, and a good view of the door. I felt I was always looking out for places with observation points and watching my back. What had happened to me in the hunt made me do this, but it was a good thing, I was always alert. I put my coat over the back of a chair and headed to the bar, got myself a bottle of Newcastle brown ale, and headed back to the table. I'd been sitting there for about fifteen minutes when she walked through the doors. I raised my arm to attract her attention and caught her eye. As she walked over I stood up – that was something my dad taught me, always respect a lady, and be a gentleman. I then headed back to the bar for the drink she had asked for. We had a quiet drink or two in the corner of the bar and after we'd finished, she asked if I would like to go to her place for a bite to eat. Yes, why not, I thought. We finished our drinks, got up and headed back to her place.

On the way we chatted about nothing much, she seemed different to when she was on the train. She asked why I had decided to ring her, but I couldn't tell her the truth, so I said I thought she was nice and I would like to get to know her, that was it. She smiled and said she thought I was a good looking man. When we got to the house, she said her house mate was out and wouldn't be back until late. She had made a hotpot, and as she opened the front door, the delicious smell hit us straight away, it smelt just like Mam's. As we walked along the hallway, she pointed out the living room. It was a very basic room, a settee against the back wall, one armchair in the window and a coffee table sat on a rug by the fire. I asked straight out if she had any drink. "Yes." She shouted though, as she had gone straight to the kitchen. "Just a moment, I'll get you one."

I sat on the chair in the window and had a good look around the room. I noticed there were no photos on display. Strange, I thought, all homes had photos in the living room. At that moment Paula came in with a can of lager in one hand and a glass in the other. "Lager OK?" she asked. "Yes, that's fine thank you." As she walked back to the kitchen I put the glass between my legs and popped the ring pull on the can. As I was pouring my drink she came in and sat on the settee with a glass of vodka and coke. We chatted about nothing much once again, what she did as a job and the travelling she had to do, mostly what she had already told me on the train. The strong, rich smell of the hotpot was making me feel hungry. After a while, Paula headed back to the kitchen and called me through, "Dinner is served".

The kitchen was a much bigger room than the living room, this was where she must spend most of her time, it was like a second living room. I commented on the room and her reply was as I thought, "My house mate likes watching the TV, me, I like to read, so I spend most of my time in here." After we had finished the hotpot we just sat chatting.

The time was getting on and I thought it only right to ask if I could stay. "You took your time, didn't you?" she said. I hoped you would be."

We headed upstairs before her house mate came back in from wherever he had been. As we got into bed, I thought she was quite a looker.

The next morning I woke about 10:00 hours but Paula wasn't in the bed beside me. I sat up and looked around. I felt a cold shiver down my spine and couldn't help but think something was going on. I jumped out of bed and was starting to put my trousers on when the bedroom door opened and in she walked with a tray. She had got up and had made us a fried breakfast. She looked at me questioningly. "You OK?" she asked, "you look as if you've had a nightmare." I could feel the sweat on my brow. "No, don't be daft," I said, but to be fair I might have as I felt on edge. This wasn't right. I was normally fine but I did feel uneasy. I got back into bed, and we sat in bed eating breakfast. It must have been about 12:00 hours when we got up and went into the living room.

When I next looked at the clock it was 13:45 hours. I got up and headed for the toilet. I looked back at her as she sat in the chair. What was I doing? This wasn't me, I thought. I wouldn't treat a lady like this. I knew I wasn't going to see her again and I felt bad. I picked up my bag and left. She must have heard the front door shut and came running out. As I walked down the street, she called out to me, but I took no notice, didn't even look back, just kept heading for the bus stop. *What a shit I was, she had done nothing but be nice to me.*

I decided to head to camp at Kirton in Lindsey. I may not get in but I had a friend that was married and I was hoping I could stay at his for the next few days.

The train journey was a good one, it seemed to go quickly, and before I knew it I was at Scunthorpe station. I got off the train and headed straight for the exit. A pub across the road caught my eye. Although I drank in Scunthorpe many times, this pub was one I hadn't been in. Dodging the traffic as I walked across the street, I noticed the front of the pub was all clear glass. There was a group of lads sitting at a window seat on the left side of the pub, nothing strange about that, or so I thought, as I pushed the two sets of doors open and walked through. Just then I heard a soft spoken northern voice, "Can I get you a drink, sir?" I turned and looked. That was not the voice I was expecting from the man that stood in front of me – he was about 6 foot 2 inches and built like a brick shithouse. However, his voice was soft and polite. "Yes, I'll have a bottle of Newcastle brown ale please." At that I dropped my bag to the floor. He bent down to the fridge behind him. "Good to hear another Geordie voice, where you from?" he said as he put the bottle on the counter. "Gateshead, you?" "Newcastle, Wallsend." "Ah, yes, I know it." "That's three of us," he said, laughing, "We could take this lot," he added jokingly, as he pointed to the lads sitting in the window. The room seemed to go quiet.

I looked around. The group of lads sitting at the window table had turned and were looking at us. I turned back to the barman thinking something was going to kick off. In his soft Geordie voice he said, "Don't worry mate, they won't start anything in here, my mate is in the back and he is the other Geordie." I picked up my bottle and started to pour it into the half tilted schooner class I had been handed from the barman. He stuck his hand out. "I'm Rob, and you are?" I looked at him, put my hand in his and said, "I'm John." Just at that point, a man walked through a door from behind the bar, he was even taller than Rob. "This is the other Geordie I was telling you about," and he pointed to the man, David. "We own the bar, and David is also the resident singer." I put my hand out to him. "Good to meet you," he said, as Rob introduced me. "What sort of songs do you sing?" I asked, genuinely interested. "Mostly from the 40s and 50s, the Rat Pack, Elvis, Buddy Holly, and Bobby Vie." He then pointed to the space just past the window where the lads were sitting. I turned to look. It was a raised area about 6ft by 6ft, with a mic stand on it. "That's my Wembley stadium," he said and started to laugh. I saw the funny side of it and had a bit smile. I felt welcome and started to relax a bit. I had a good look around the bar, at the paintings on the walls, small captions on them. One that caught my eye was a distorted face that had a death look about it, blood dripping from a badly cut eye, and the caption: *Good Win*, with pound signs floating up from the face. I didn't get it so I turned to Rob and asked if he knew what it meant. "No mate, I was just asked to draw it."

"So *you* do them?" I said, amazed.

"Yes, it's a hobby of mine, I think it was one of the lads sitting over there." He pointed to them in the window seat. "They are doormen from the club down the road."

The penny dropped. Doormen, death, and cash. A cold shivering feeling surged through my body and I started to feel uneasy.

David had been setting up his stage for tonight's show, and as he came back to the bar, he looked at me. "You OK mate?" he said, "you've gone white." Rob also looked, "Do you need a drink of water?"

"No mate, I'm fine, this happens to me a bit, but the doctor hasn't a clue what it is, I'll be fine in a moment." Where that came from I didn't know, but I'm pleased I said it, I couldn't get the lads in the window seat out of my head, they had to have been on the hunt, or had been on one in the past. Would I recognise any of them, or more to the point would any of them recognise *me*? I had to decide, should I stay and finish my drink or leave? I tried to keep my back to them, but if they were going to recognise me, they would have. When I crossed the road, when I walked in the pub, or when they all looked over as Rob said we could take them. I took a big gamble and stayed. I ordered another bottle of brown ale and sat chatting with Rob. David had gone back to the 'stage' as he called it.

A little later, David returned to the bar and started to go through some drawers. Rob asked what he was after.

"I've snapped one of the wires and I need some tape to repair it."

Rob opened a drawer beside him. "Will this do?" he asked, as he pulled out a roll of Sellotape.

"No, it has to be masking tape."

"No David," I said, "I can fix it with that." I took it out of Rob's hand and walked over to the stage. None of the lads in the window seat took any notice, they just sat chatting. As

I started to repair the wire David joined me, I then heard one of the lads say the linking lads hadn't come back yet. I worked slowly and quietly so I could hear every word they said. "That has to be over two weeks by now," another said. "No," another piped up, "about three to four weeks." "Yes, but even that is a long time, something must have gone wrong, the most it takes is six days."

I was right, they have been on hunts in the past, but it seemed not this one. I had to try and find out more, but how? I finished repairing the wire and walked back to the bar with David. "Give him the next bottle on the house," he said to Rob. "No, there's no need for that, I'm glad to help." "No, *we* are glad for the help, if David isn't on that stage tonight the girls will go off it, that's all they come in for." We laughed. David had gone a bit red in the face. Time went on and I had one or two more bottles. Finally, the lads in the window seat got up and walked out. As they left Rob held his hand up and said "See you tomorrow lads." Yes, one of them said. They all seemed to give a little wave saying see you mate. As the door closed behind them, Rob and David said at the same time, WANKERS. It was clear then they didn't like them. "I take it they're not your mates," I said. "If it wasn't for them spending a lot of money in here, we wouldn't let them in. They're troublemakers, not in here, but we have heard some poor young lads have suffered at the hands of them." This was interesting. They had to be part of the hunters.

"So, what sort of things?"

Rob stopped David saying any more. "Sorry mate, we can't say anymore, it would be more than our lives are worth."

"No problem mate, I understand." I was onto something

here but how could I find out more? After I'd finished my bottle, I shook hands with them and said I had to be off, I said I would pop back with some of my mates if that was OK. Of course, the more the merrier, came the reply. With that I picked up my bag and left.

I walked down the street to where Rob had pointed earlier as he said the lads worked at the club down the street. About 200 yards down, I saw a club – this had to be the one, The Scunthorpe Palace it was called. I walked past, having a quick look at the entrance, nothing unusual. I noticed no back lane down the side and got a bad feeling as I thought back to the kicking I'd got with Brit and Kenny in Lincolnshire. I started to feel nerves as I slowed down to take things in. I thought it had to have a back entrance. I had walked about 30 to 40 minutes before I spotted a back lane heading between two old closed down shops. I looked down it, it had to go to the back of the club. Would I walk down it now or wait until I had some of the lads with me? I turned and looked up the other side of the street. I noticed a hotel opposite the club. That was it, I had three days left until I had to return to camp. I walked to the hotel and asked the receptionist if I could have a room that looked over the street. She looked through the book before saying, "We only have one left on the top floor, if that will do you, sir."

"That's fine love, is the bar open?"

"Yes, sir, down the hall and on the right."

I booked in and headed for the bar ...

Great, the bar looked out onto the street, this was just down from the entrance to the club. I sat by the window and had a pint, thinking what I might see, if anything. Would I recognise anyone, or would this turn out to be a waste of time? I had to try, even just to put my mind at rest. After I finished my pint, I headed to my room checking the fire exit as an escape route just in case it was needed.

I took my time opening the door, I had started to feel uneasy again. Why I didn't know, maybe because I was on my own, I had no backup, and I wouldn't be missed for a while if something was to happen to me. I pushed the door open and stood back – nothing. A window was straight ahead of the door. I walked in, put my bag on the bed and looked out of the window. It was covered with a net certain, ideal for looking out through the day, but at night I would have to draw the curtains and leave a small gap to look through. I looked over the road, the club entrance was directly ahead of my room. This would be great. The time now was 16:45 hours and I decided to get my head down for a while. I phoned reception and asked if they could give me a wake-up call at 19:30 hours, and have a meal delivered at the same time. Yes, sir that would be fine, what would I like to eat? Steak pie, mash and veg please, not a problem, sir, leave that with me and I will ensure it is done. I put the phone down, took my shoes off and lay on top of the bed. It felt so soft, I felt I could stay there until the end of time. My thoughts strayed to Brit and Kenny…

A piercing ring. I grabbed the receiver and cried, "Who are you? What do you want?"

A young girl's voice answered, "It is the call you requested, sir, the time is 19:30, sir."

"Sorry about that," I said, suddenly remembering where I was.

"It's OK, sir, are you happy with your stay so far, sir?"

"Yes, great thanks," I muttered.

"Your meal will be with you in five minutes, sir."

I then put the receiver down and looked out of the window. The sun was starting to go down over buildings and the street was now full of people dressed for a night out. The club over the road was now open and there were three men on the door. No one going in at the moment, a bit early for clubbers, I thought. I jumped in the shower, and enjoyed the hot water running down my back. I started to feel relaxed and loose; I was obviously still bruised all over my back and as the water hit my skin it stung a bit, but at the same time it felt invigorating.

Glenn Harwood

(Glenn)

Royal Artillery
1978 to 1984

After my shower, I popped the kettle on while I dried myself. A knock at the door startled me. "Room service" a voice called out. I opened the door and a young girl stood there with a trolley. I only had a towel around my waist. She pushed in the trolley and as she walked out she said, "Enjoy, sir," without looking at me. I think it was a bit embarrassing for her.

I sat on the end of the bed and ate the meal. Outside it was starting to get dark and I closed the curtains. I then sat back on the end of the bed, drinking my tea, thinking of the picture on the wall in the pub I had been in earlier that day. I hadn't even got the name of it. I got up again and looked out of the window to the club. There were now people going in, and it wouldn't be too long before people started to get put out. Checking my watch I saw it was now 21:30 hours. Down the street was a chippy. The meal I'd had didn't seem to fill me, so I had time to get some supper before anything would happen.

I stayed on the opposite side of the street from the club, I didn't want to attract attention to myself, and was hoping none of the doormen would see me or recognise me. While I stood in the chippy waiting for the fish to be fried, two young lads came in, being loud and boisterous. The woman behind the counter asked them to calm it down, and one of them told her to fuck off as she gave him his chips. There was only the one woman and two young girls working in the shop.

"That's it, out you go, you're not getting served!"

The lads thought they were so funny. They grabbed the salt and vinegar and threw them at the young woman. I turned and looked at them, "Come on lads, there's no need for this." I tried to calm things down.

One of the lads grabbed me by the throat, but before he had time to lift a hand to hit me, he was on the floor, with his nose all over his face. His friend turned towards me looking surprised, and without thinking up came my leg, a roundhouse kick to the head, and down he went too. Then I dragged the two of them out into the street. This was not what I wanted, I needed to keep a low profile. I walked back into the chippy and asked if my fish was ready.

"Yes, sir, and thank you for that."

"Don't mention it," I said, as I picked up my fish and chips and left.

I had planned on heading back to the hotel, but now I just wanted to get away from the area. I headed back down the street, towards the pub I had been in that afternoon. I got to the station and sat on a park bench to eat my supper. As I sat I kept looking up the street, hoping the two lads I had just put to sleep wouldn't head this way. I looked over the road and saw that the pub was called Good Brewers. I had heard of it before, or something similar, but from where I couldn't remember. I finished my supper and headed to the pub for a pint before heading back to the hotel. Rob was behind the bar with two young girls, and David was on his stage blasting out a Frank Sinatra song. The pub was quite full and as I walked to the bar, Rob got his eye on me. He mouthed Newky broon and I gave him the thumbs up. When I got to the bar, I handed him a £5 note, sat on a stool at the corner of the counter, with my back to a wall – it made me feel happy and safe that no one could get behind me. Once David had finished the first half of his turn, he came over and sat with me.

"You're not bad at it, are you mate?" he said, smiling.

"I try."

"I wasn't expecting to see you so soon back in the pub mate."

"No, I hadn't intended coming back so soon either mate, but I had to get out of the hotel for a while."

"You here for long?"

"Am looking for work, but not sure if I'll stay in the area."

The painting that had caught my eye earlier, was in front of me, I was sure I'd seen it before, from where I couldn't say. I asked David about the lads that had been in the bar in the afternoon. "You were going to tell me something about them, what was it mate?"

David looked at the bar, to see if Rob was watching. As he did so Rob gave him a look as if to say *don't you dare*. David turned with a red face, "It was nothing," he said. I knew there was something but what I didn't want to push him for. I finished my drink and headed back to the hotel.

When I got to my room, I left the light off, pulled a chair over to the window and sat by it. There were three doormen at the door as earlier, it was now 22:30 hours, and plenty of life in the street. People went in and out of the club with no trouble, everything was as normal as could be. A fight started outside the club, the doormen just stood and watched, they seemed to just have a laugh at the lads fighting, not much of a fight, more handbags at dawn. There was nothing to see tonight and I was starting to wonder if I was wasting my time. Was I trying to find something that wasn't even there?

It had turned 03:00 hours and the club was starting to empty, lots of shouting and singing, but nothing more. I turned in for the night, the painting from Good Brewers was still bugging me. I had set the alarm on my watch for 06:00 hours and turned over.

I awoke with the sound of the alarm, it couldn't possibly be time to get up, I felt as though I had just nodded off. I got up, headed for the window and drew back the curtain; the sun was bright and stung my eyes. After rubbing them to try and clear them, I looked out and the street was covered in old fish and chip papers, the odd puddle of vomit.

After showering, I got dressed and headed down to the lobby, it was a bright, sunny morning, the birds were singing and the air was fresh. I walked over the road to the front of the club, avoiding the sick and chip papers, turned right and headed up the street. About 150 yards up there was a back alley. I took a slow walk down it. I took my time, having a good look around, and then I was at the back of the club. It had a big yard, with a lot of empty beer crates and kegs stacked up to the right side, to the left was a small table and four chairs – this must be where the doormen have a coffee on their break – on the opposite side of the alley there were high walls to what looked like office buildings, nothing more to look at, there was nothing else I could see that would help me, or anything I could check out the back of the club from.

I headed back to the hotel for my breakfast and on the way I called to a paper shop, grabbed a paper and a packet of chewing gum. On the front page was a story about a group of men from Lincolnshire that had gone missing from work; they all worked at a night club, and hadn't been seen for over two weeks, none of the families had heard from them, the club manager had said they'd all left the club together on the night they disappeared, and none of them have been seen since. The police were asking the public to look out for the cars they had travelled in, they gave a description of the men and the cars – this was the lot that had taken us to the Yorkshire moors and who had tried to kill us. From this I took it the police and the SAS still had them, and the cars had been left in the huts. This got me thinking back to the note that I'd found in my pocket at the train station, RUN. Someone, somewhere knew about this and I still couldn't work out if I should be running or it all was a sick joke.

As I sat having breakfast, I wondered how Kenny and Brit were doing. Kenny's eye had been a mess after he got Brit to cut it, and I knew Glenn was going to take him on one of his survival sessions, if he had got out of hospital in time, and he wouldn't go easy on him. As Glenn always said, to survive you have to be tough and no matter what, you get on with it. Brit had taken Dunc to London with him, and was working on Dunc staying in the group. Jock and Platty there was no question about them staying with the group, they loved this kind of thing, but me, I was starting to think too deep into everything. I need the lads, especially Bob and Tony, they would sort me. They had a way of getting you to think in the right way. After breakfast I had decided I was not staying around here, I had to head back to camp. If I stayed around I may get into trouble and that wouldn't be good for me or the group.

The camp opened on the Saturday ready for the lads heading back. Tony and the lads had a good leave after they got over thinking about what we had all been though. I stayed at my mates for the rest of my leave and after, I decided to go into camp on the Sunday. Most of the lads would be heading back to camp the same day.

It felt good to be in camp, why I didn't know, but I felt safe, it must have been knowing the lads would be back soon and we could get down to business. Tony was the first one to walk into the accommodation. The smile on my face when I saw him was from ear to ear. We hugged and I felt I had to thank him again for what he and the lads had done for me – after all, they had saved my life. Me, Kenny and Brit owed them our lives. We headed to his room put the kettle on and chatted about what we had been doing on leave, and what we had thought about being part of group, we could hear doors going and people coming and going; some of the lads from the battery had returned, but we hadn't heard voices at this point. We were listening for Brit and the rest of the lads.

Tony decided we should go to the NAAFI for a pint. As we were leaving his room, Jock and Glenn were just walking into the block. They stopped and dropped their bags, Glenn held out his arms. I know it sounds sloppy, but we meant that much to each other. I walked straight to him and we hugged, glad to see you Geordie he said. I turned to jock, looked him in the eyes, thank you mate. I turned back to Glenn, to thank him. He looked me in the eye, "Don't you fuckin' dare!" My eyes were full. "Don't you bloody *dare* thank me," he said. "We are a *family*, and families stick together ... so don't you dare!" and he hugged me again. Jock piped up, "Give up with the slavers, let's go for a pint."

The four of us set off to the NAAFI. When we arrived Glenn pushed the doors open. Sitting at the far end of the bar were Brit and Dunc, a pint in one hand and a tab in the other. "Come on lads, where the hell have you been?" They had to have been there for some time. As Brit was half cut, off we went again with the hugs. I got the pints in and we sat at a table, we started chatting about what we had said to friends and family, none of them had said a word, all they had spoken about was the Falklands. Glenn started telling us about his and Kenny's last week of leave, on what they call, their 'survival training'. As I thought, Kenny had pushed himself and Glenn wouldn't let him stop, to them pain was a sensation and sensations don't last, so enjoy them while they're there. We had probably sank about 6 or 7 pints each before we headed off to bed; we all felt good about ourselves, and for some reason we couldn't wait to get started on the next task. We all said goodnight and I headed to my room, popped the kettle on and took out the biscuits from the back of my sock drawer. As I was pouring the tea, my door opened and in walked Glenn. "I'll have one mate," he said, as he sat on the bed. "I thought I should check what you've decided to tell the lads." "What do you mean?" I couldn't think what he was on about. "You, Brit and Kenny went AWOL for two days before leave, and the lads are going to ask questions." I hadn't even thought about it.

"I spoke to Kenny and we think you should say that you went off with Catton." "What do you mean *we went off with Catton?*" "When we all left the club, Catton picked up a lass, so we think you should say you, Kenny and Brit went off with him, and three other lasses, and stayed at one of the lass's houses. I'll speak with Brit, and in the morning I'll catch BSM Bob at the gate before he takes the parade, what do you think mate?" "I suppose we'll have to say something, we can't say anything about what really happened until we speak with BSM Bob." We drank the tea and chatted for a while longer, before Glenn got up off the bed. We shook hands and hugged; the grip we had felt special. I knew if at any time I was in trouble, Glenn would be there, the whole team had risked their lives for me, so I felt special. To think I hadn't known them for long, but they had done that for me and it meant a lot. Glenn left and headed to speak with Brit.

The next morning we all headed for breakfast. When you got up, you did your own thing. I would be up about 05:30 hours, go for a run, back for a shower, then breakfast. However, this morning was different. I hadn't set the alarm, but still got up as usual 5:30 hours. I sat up in bed, and started thinking what was going to happen from now on. Life was going to be different, although we were still part of the regiment, we had become a team, a special team, one that wouldn't – couldn't – be broken. We would stand together through thick and thin.

I binned the run, had a cup of tea, then went off for my shower. 08:00 hours we would all gather outside the block, stand around until one of us would spot BSM Bob, then the duty sergeant would get us on parade. I saw Glenn running along the road. I reckon he had seen BSM Bob, and needed to get to the parade before Bob turned up. As Bob was walking along the path, I looked at him. I could see Tony and Glenn doing the same. What we got was not what we expected.

"*FACE THE FRONT YOU HORRIBLE BUNCH OF MEN!*"

But to be fair he couldn't give any of the other lads a clue what we had been through; he had to treat us no different to the rest. After he called out everyone's name, and checked we were all present and correct, and informed us that Catton had left the army, he then looked at me and Brit.

"Yes, they're back, sir," said the duty sergeant. Taking an extra two or three days leave didn't go unnoticed, making it look as if nothing had gone on.

"I will see you two later," he said as he dismissed us.

The rest of the lads started to ask questions to find out where we had gone. I was thinking whether to stick to Glenn's story or not, when Platty piped up, "You scruffy twats, picking up slappers from Scunny." The lads all started to laugh. "We all know," Platty said, "Glenn told us you and Catton had gone off together."

I looked at Glenn, a little wink came back. I said, "No you're wrong." Brit and Glenn looked surprised, thinking I was going to change the story. "No, Brit had the slapper, my one was not bad." They all just kept taking the micky as we walked to the garages.

Glenn and Tony headed to the gym where Kenny was. When we arrived at the garage, the troop sergeant gave us jobs for the day, the norm – strip the Land Rovers, clean them and put them back together, lay out the cam nets, repair the holes. I don't know how, but every time you got the nets out, there seemed to be more holes, even if you hadn't used them. 10:00 hours was NAFFI break. Just as we started to set off, the troop sergeant stopped us, got us on parade.

"Right lads, I have a task that needs six bodies, volunteers required, step forward." No one ever stepped forward. "Right," he said, "I'll pick you, you two and you." He pointed at me, Brit and Dunc. "Right, three more." Donny, Jock and Platty were the next three he pointed at. I knew then it was the BSM that wanted us, the rest of the lads headed for the NAFFI.

When we arrived at the office door, it was ajar. I knocked. "WAIT," came a loud deep voice from behind the door. BSM Bob had the nickname, Bob the Gob, and it fitted. We had been standing at the door for about five minutes, before the voice boomed again. "ENTER." We walked in and Bob was sat behind his desk, to the right were two men, and around from them were nine chairs to the left of the desk. "Come in and sit down lads, shut the door Jock." As we did, Bob introduced Captain Jones of the SAS, the one on the left, and Detective Anderson of the Metropolitan Police. I had sat next to him. I looked at the two of them, said hello, then looked back at Bob. Captain Jones called out, "You're looking a lot better than you did the last time I saw you." He was speaking to me. Donny nodded toward him. I turned to him, "Sorry, sir," I said, "I didn't realise you were speaking to me. Yes, sir, I feel a lot better thanks."

He looked at Brit. "You too lad?"

"Yes, sir, I'm feeling great, thanks to my mates. If it wasn't for this lot I probably wouldn't be here."

"Yes, they've done you proud," he said. Just at that point there was a knock on the door.

"COME IN," Bob boomed, and in walked Tony, Glenn and Kenny.

Bob had phoned the gym earlier and asked them to attend.

"Take a seat lads, we have things to talk about."

Bob started by saying the night at the club where it all started for us all, was not the full story and it had a lot more to it. Captain Jones was going to speak with us all, but before he did, he had something to say.

"As you know, I'm very proud of you all, you did well from start to finish. I take it you're all up for the team?" He looked at Dunc, he knew Dunc had had doubts about staying as part of the team.

"Yes, sir, I'm up for it."

"What changed your mind?"

"I went on leave with Britnell, and we saw some doormen giving a young lad a good kicking, the lad had no chance, but they didn't give a shit. This needs to be stopped, and if I can help stop it, I will."

The rest of us said yes to the team.

"That's good," he said, "but one thing has changed … I am out."

SHIT! we thought, would that be the end of it?

"Don't worry," he said, "it is still on. I'll be running things from camp, but will not be going out with you all. We thought we'd need one more for the team, but we think two would be better, so start thinking who you think it could be. I'll now hand you over to Captain Jones."

Andrew Evans

(Evo)

Royal Artillery, 1980 to 1999

"Good day lads, I will start by saying BSM is right, you have done a fantastic job, and that's why we are here, we think you have stumbled on something big, as we informed you back at Hereford we believe this is country wide; we think they have been doing this for years, but have been doing it with big gaps, moving around the country for their targets. We still have them all at Hereford. Out of the 21 we have, 14 are dead, three are still in a bad way, and four of them are fine. Three of the four have spoken, they say it is only the second time this has happened. We don't believe this, one of them has given us more than the other two, we have done a deal with him, for his freedom and no charges against him. He informed us that there were two more on the hunt, that had got away from it all, with the help of the police. There was a man found partly buried in a wood near the moors, he has been identified as one of the hunters. The one that's gone missing was the one they called Big Bob, it turns out he double-crossed them by taking off with the cash prize. We have been looking for him for the last week, but he has gone to ground. The men we have came from five locations around the country, so you will have to try and find him. Of course we'll help but from here, Big Bob could be anywhere as he has friends all around the country, and probably more of the underworld than the rest of them put together.

So we're hoping you can find out more. If any of you can think of anything you may have heard at the club before it all started, or while you were locked up at the huts..." (as he looked at me, Brit and Kenny) "...it may not seem much, but it may help."

The met officer piped up, "We know it is in the papers, but it has been put to one side, my officers have been informed, only speak of it when the reporters ask questions, all they will say is it's being investigated."

I stuck my hand up and Captain Jones pointed to me.

"Go ahead, Gordon."

Flippin' heck, he knew my name.

"While I was on leave I went home to see my parents."

"Yes you did, and ended up speaking with one of my old mates from the SAS, didn't you?"

No way! Freddy had shit on me. I couldn't lie, that was one thing my dad had always said, no matter what shit you're in, never lie.

"Yes, sir, I did." I could see the lads weren't happy. "I have known him for years, sir, he put me through a lot of training before I joined up, and helped me with survival training."

"Don't worry, yes, you shouldn't have spoken with anyone, but Freddy has informed me all about what you went through as a kid, and how much you relied on him for help, get back to your story."

"Well, when I left home I made my way back to Scunthorpe, and stayed in a hotel just along the street from the train station, but as I got off the train I headed for Good Brewers, it's a pub across the road from the station, sir. I sat at the bar having a pint. In one of the window seats was a bunch of lads, I got chatting to the two lads that own the pub, they're both from Newcastle. As we chatted I noticed some paintings on the walls, there wasn't anything to them, except one of them. It was a strange looking painting of a face, it had a badly cut eye, blood dripping from it, it also had pound signs floating up from it. I had seen one similar somewhere before, but where I can't remember. Anyhow, it was one of the doormen that got him, that is Rob, one of the barmen to draw it. He didn't tell him why, but he was adamant it had to have the pound signs in it and blood drops from the one eye."

Tony called out that it was at the club in Lincolnshire, in the entrance hall behind the cloakroom stuff on the back wall.

"It sounds very similar. OK, lads," the police officer said, "There might be a link. This could be one place to start."

Captain Jones had the last word, "Are you all up for it?"

A resounding yes was the reply from us all.

"OK, one or two things are a must, *none* of you is to speak about this to anyone, you are now the team and will be called up at any time, so always have your kit ready. Your tasks will be given to you from BSM Bob, as you call him. We need the club in Scunthorpe checked out, and you all keep out of trouble. We are informing the regiment that you're a training team for the SAS to hunt down, so they will be informed that you can be in civilian clothes or uniform, so as far as anyone will know you're on exercise. Any questions?"

"Yes, sir," Glenn said, "Can we end it at any time? I mean, if we catch any of them, and we get put into a tight situation?"

"You do what you think is the right thing at the time, but remember it is a civilian situation that you're working in, and the local police could also be involved in the same task, just be careful."

Captain Jones and Detective Anderson said goodbye to us all and wished us good luck.

"Remember one thing boys," Detective Anderson said, "you're on your own if things go wrong."

As they left, Bob got Kenny to put the kettle on and got

Tony to pop next door and get some biscuits from the duty clerk. I got up and gave Kenny a hand with tea, Bob opened the top drawer of his desk, pulled out a folder and dropped it on the desk. I handed the tea out and we sat back down. Bob opened the folder and got us to keep the noise down while he started to tell us of what he had planned, things had changed slightly after I had given them what I had seen in Scunthorpe.

"Right lads, I've decided we need three teams of four, known as a brick, so we are now in need of three more bodies. Before I forget, Geordie, you will be getting a new room mate at the weekend, McVaigh. He is coming from Woolwich, so look after him."

"No problem, sir, but if he is sharing a room with me, do you not think we should look at him as one of the team? It would make sense, and that way I wouldn't have to keep making excuses for me keep disappearing."

"OK, we'll see how he is when he arrives, so let's concentrate on the other two for now."

Brit wanted to know about Evo, that's Andy Evans. "He is good in the field, and has a tendency to keep out of trouble but observes well."

"Yes," Bob said, "we could look at him. One more lads."

"Mark Smeeton," Tony suggested. "What about him?"

He was one that didn't look like a squaddie, but he was fit and on the ball. Bob agreed we'd look at them over the next two weeks.

"Geordie, you tell us about that pub you went in," Bob said, "the one by the train station, what was it called?"

"Good Brewers, sir, the two lads that run it are the owners, and they are both Geordies, sir, one of them was ready to tell me about the doormen and I think the painting, that was David. Rob, the other one, he is the painter, there was something he wasn't telling me, he seemed to be scared of something, he might know something about what is going on."

"Right then, that's where we'll start, we need to sort out teams, for when and if it comes to working in teams, but for now we work together and as *one* team. Tony, you will have team Alfa, with Donny and Jock for now, Geordie you have team Bravo, with Platty for now. Glenn, Charlie with Kenny and Dunc, Delta, with Brit. We'll see what the other three are like, and I may have to change things around. Right, for the two lads at Good Brewers, Geordie, you, Tony and Glenn go down tonight, have a good chat with them, take photos of all the paintings if you get the chance, we need to know as much as possible about the doormen and the painting. Was it David that was going to tell you stuff?"

"Yes, sir."

"Then work on him. Kenny and Dunc, you go in the pub about 21:00 hours and meet up with them, don't push them too hard, we don't want them getting nervous about the situation. Donny, you take Brit, Platty and Jock, sit away from them, but close enough so you can hear what is going on … and if there is a group of lads in that look like doormen, get as close as you can to them."

We all stood up, gave a 'Yes, sir' or an 'OK' to him as we left, and as we walked down the stairs, I called out to Tony and Glenn informing them I would meet them at the camp gates that evening at 19:00 hours. The rest of the lads had decided to meet at the Scunthorpe Arms, and have a drink there before heading to Good Brewers.

We all then went back to the garage while Tony, Glenn and Kenny returned to the gym. I got on with sorting out the cam nets, and when I had finished, I packed them away, and set off to give Dunc a hand with the Land Rover; he had the back wheels off. I walked over to him and told him the BSM wanted him in his office. He got up and started to put the tools away. As I said this, Brit was at the Land Rover next to him, he looked at me and started to laugh. Dunc looked at him, then looked back at me. I had a big grin on my face. "You twat!" The penny dropped, it was what he had done to me when I first joined the regiment, except he and Brit set about me, to test me out. He then joined us laughing.

"I'll get you for that you Geordie twat, and you can stop laughing you cockney shit."

It was great to think we had become such close friends, I felt like I was really part of something, for the first time in my life I had started to belong to something real.

John Hughes

(Jock)

Royal Artillery, 1981 to 1990

As we started to clear away the jobs, Donny came over and informed me he was going to head to Good Brewers with his lads at about 20:15 hours. "We're all going to the pub counter so we can have a good look around, we won't speak to you, and tell your lads to not speak to us mate."

"OK, no problem mate, but remember if things go wrong, we'll be there for you if needed."

I was walking to my room when Evo caught up with me. "Hi Geordie, how's it going mate?"

"All OK mate, did you have a good leave?"

"Yes, not bad mate. Listen, what's going on mate? You and a few of the lads are up to something."

"Don't know what you mean mate." I tried to take him away from what he was after.

"Listen, I have to put a football team together, do you fancy playing? It's over six games, it's with the RAF and the Gunners."

"Yes mate, put me down for it."

"Can I get you to get four more players, I'm still looking for four more players."

As we headed to the cookhouse for tea, Evo reeled off name after name. I wasn't interested in the football team but I needed to get him off the scent that something was going on, even though he may become one of the team later on. I couldn't say anything about what I was up to.

While we queued for tea, Evo saw one of the lads he was hoping would join the football team. "I'll see you later Geordie," he said as he set off over to speak with him.

In the cookhouse, I spotted Kenny sitting at the opposite side of the room and he waved me over. We chatted about nothing much while we ate. He didn't seem to be himself, rather quiet for him, he was normally joking around, but he seemed subdued. I thought I should speak with Glenn and Tony that night, they would know how to get through to him. When we'd finished our meal, I headed back to my room, had a shower and got myself dressed for the night. As I was locking my room door, I saw Dunc walking along the corridor. "You going out for a smoke mate?"

"Yes, you?"

"Yes" and he handed me a tab as we walked. We then sat on a seat in front of the accommodation, the sun was starting to go down, and as it did it glittered through the trees and the warm rays hit my face. I relaxed back into the seat. I had ten minutes before I had to head to the camp gates to meet up with Glenn and Tony. Dunc had decided to wait until 19:15 hours until he would meet up with Brit and the rest of the lads. As we sat Dunc asked what I thought of it all. Before I had time to answer, he said he was glad he'd decided to stay with the group. "So am I," I said, "you all mean so much to me."

"What do you mean?" he wanted to know.

I started to tell him about my time at school and my first job, the bullying and dyslexia. He didn't believe me but time was getting on. I stood up and said I'd have a chat with him another time. I had to go. "See you later, and keep out of trouble," I said.

"*Me?* Never in trouble," and he started to smile, with the look on his face of a man that could fool anyone.

I then headed to the gates to meet up with Tony and Glenn. As I approached Tony and Glenn were already there, and the taxi was waiting on the road outside the gates. Glenn called out, "Come on fat boy," as I started to jog. Glenn had names for everyone that didn't work in the gym. To be fair, I was probably fat compared to him, he was in the best shape you could possibly wish for. I got in the car after them, just my luck, I was in the front seat. Tony had always said, the man in the front seat pays. I just had to make sure I got in the back on the way back. I got the taxi to drop us outside the hotel, just along the street from Good Brewers. When I got out the taxi, I put my hand into my front pocket and pulled a fiver out and handed it to the driver. I looked over the road, and as luck would have it, one of the doormen that had been in Good Brewers the other day, was heading down the street in the direction of Brewers.

Steven Platt

(Platty)

Royal Artillery, 1980 to 1987

I called to Tony and Glenn, "Check him out lads, he is one of the doormen I told you about." Tony started to go red in the face. "Calm down mate," Glenn said, "we have to do this right." Tony turned to me. "I didn't think I would feel like this when I saw them, it just brings it back what they did to you on the moors." He started to take deep breaths. Glenn said, "You need to control it mate, we all want to give them a good kicking, but we can't, so hold it together mate." Tony calmed down, "Sorry lads, you're right, I'll try and hold it together."

"Let's just take our time down the road lads," I said.

At this point Glenn stopped. "Is that the club they work at?" I nodded. "Then let's have a look around before it opens."

"I've had a look, nothing to see," I said.

"Well, let's check anyway."

We headed up the street away from Good Brewers and stopped by a row of shops. Sitting on a bench we looked over towards the club and the back alley down the side of it. Tony decided to walk over the road and take a slow walk down the alley, while me and Glenn just sat observing the layout of the area. After about ten minutes we saw Tony walking up the street in front of the club.

"How the hell did he get there?" I said. The alley had no way out at the bottom that I could see. Glenn laughed, "You're not as observant as you thought." Tony walked back over the road and sat back on the bench. Without pointing or looking over to the club he said, "Can you see that office building on the right of the alley? It has a fire escape ladder at the back of it, and a platform at the top, we can observe the back of the club from there, and halfway down the alley is a small archway leading to the street. Those are the only two I can see that could help us if we have to stake out the place."

"What good's the alley if it's down the street?" queried Glenn.

I jumped in, "We can have men at the front of the street, close to it, just in case things kick off." Tony agreed.

We got up and headed down the street, towards Good Brewers. As we walked Glenn and Tony were observing everything on and around the street looking for observation points, good cover areas and places to have men in waiting as back up, if this was one place we'd have to send a team to.

When we reached the pub I noticed a group of men sitting in the window seat, it was the same group that had been there the last time I was in. I opened the door and stood back to let Tony and Glenn walk in first. I closed the door behind me and headed in through the second set of doors. At the bar was a group of young lads and lasses having a laugh among themselves, there was no sign of David or Rob, just two young girls serving. Glenn got to the bar first and ordered the drinks, there was no need to ask what we wanted, we always drank the same. I had a Fosters and Tony had a cider, Glenn got his normal, a bitter. As he was being served I asked one of the young girls if David was at work that evening. Yes was the reply, due to start at 9 o'clock. I said I was hoping to see him, and I'd catch him later. Rob wouldn't be back until Thursday, she told me. She thought he'd gone home for a few days – back to Newcastle.

We took our pints and then sat at a table to the left of the bar; Glenn sat facing the door, and Tony sat opposite him. I sat to the side of them. I picked up my pint and said in a soft voice, "See the group of lads in the window seat?" Glenn looked over the top of his glass as he was taking a sip of his drink, Tony had his back to them, so he just looked at me. "I'll look later," he said. Glenn put his pint back on the table, "Well, who are they?" he said.

"The doormen from the club up the street."

Nothing was said.

Glenn picked up his pint again and, aiming at Tony, started speaking from behind it. "Five of them all together, two of them had to be about 6ft 2, one's about 5ft 5, but is as wide as he's tall, the last two are average height." Glenn then started to scan the bar, a fire door stood to the back of him, the gents was at the right of the bar, and the ladies just past the window seat where the five doormen sat. I looked at the pictures on the wall again. I held my pint up and told Tony that the picture I'd been on about was in the centre of the back wall. Tony turned slowly. "We need a pic of it before the night is over."

We had been sitting for about forty-five minutes before I got up to get the next round in. As the young lass was serving me, I saw the door behind the bar open. David had come down to set up the stage for his evening spot of song. He spotted me. "Hi mate," he said with a smile on his face. "I didn't expect you back so soon."

"Me neither mate, but I was down having a drink with a couple of my mates so I thought I'd pop in, and they hadn't been in here before so it is a change for them."

David looked over to the table where I'd been pointing as I was telling him this.

"Is them your mates?"

"Yes," I said as I picked up the drinks, "pop over when

you get a minute and I'll introduce you to them." I headed back to the table without saying anything more. I didn't want to seem pushy and get him on the back foot, so I just made it seem the normal thing to do.

When I sat down Glenn was looking at the entrance door. "Don't look but Donny has just walked in – *on his own.*"

We didn't expect that, him on his own. Donny walked to the bar and asked for a pint of lager, he hadn't even looked over to us. After he had been served, he sat on a bar stool at the corner of the bar, his back to the wall, about 7ft away from us and looking directly at the entrance. He didn't look out of place, every bar I had ever been in always seemed to have a punter sat at the end of the bar. Just then David came from behind the bar and headed to his stage. As he did the doormen got up.

TheGulf

Mark Smeeton

(Smeet)

Royal Artillery, 1975 to 1999

"Time to leave lads," one of them said, "the town crier is about to start." They all had a bit of a giggle, as did David. "See you tomorrow mate," one of them said to David. The door closed behind them as they headed up the street.

As David set up his stage, we decided to leave it for the night. If we started to ask questions about the doormen, he might get a bit suspicions. We stood up as David came over.

"You not leaving mate?" he said.

"Yes, but we'll pop back through the week mate."

"No you're not, I haven't had a drink with you yet, and you haven't introduced me to your mates." He called to the young lass behind the bar, "Shannon, give the lads a drink on the house, I'll be back after a couple of songs" and off he went to his stage.

I looked at the lads, "Well, what do you think lads?"

"Sit your ass down," Glenn said, "this could be the chance to find out about the doormen, *and* it's a free drink." Tony laughed. "Out for nowt," I said. Donny then looked at me for the first time, stood up and sank the last little bit of his drink, and headed to the toilet. I followed.

When I got there he was standing at the urinal, there was no one else in there. I stood next to him, he had a quick look around.

"I'm off and I'll stop the rest of the lads coming in, you get what you can from that lad, and we'll keep an eye on the club for the rest of the night."

That was what they did, but didn't get anything, apart from seeing the doormen were the same as them from Lincoln, bully boys, digging the odd young lad as they put them out the club, for whatever had gone on in the club.

THE SET UP

David sang about four or five songs, then came over. He called to Shannon for a bottle of broon ale as he sat down. Straight away Tony put out his hand. "I'm Tony mate, Geordie is quite an ignorant twat." Dave and Glenn laughed as Glenn then stood up and put out his hand. I said "This is Glenn" before he said the same and we had a bit of a giggle. "I'm David, nice to meet you both."

"What brought you down here from the north?" Glenn wanted to know.

"Well, me and my mate Rob – he's having two or three days back home at the moment – we worked for a friend back north, he has a string of coffee shops across the northeast and he was offered a night club at a good price, so he left us running the coffee shops, while he and his wife came down and got things going."

"I thought you said the pub was yours and Rob's," I said.

"It is, once my mate got a string of clubs, he ended up with seven of them, and for all the work we did for him, he paid for this pub for us.

This was interesting. He had seven night clubs. I was now wondering if he had anything to do with the hunts. "So who is this mate of yours?" Glenn asked, "I would like to meet him, he might buy *me* one." David laughed and said, "You can, he's coming down at the weekend." I could see Glenn's head ticking over, was he the one that sets the hunts up? We'd find out at the weekend, if we got the chance to come down. That shouldn't be a problem, once BSM Bob found out about this he'd ensure we got the time. This could be big, we could get in with him, try to make good friends and try to get in on the inside.

"What is it you do?" Dave then asked Glenn.

Tony Watt

Serviced 1975 to 1998
Royal Artillery, 1975 to 1990
Army Physical Training Corp, 1990 to 1998
Specialist Instruction Officer
(None Regular Permanent Staff)
1998 to still serving 2020

"Me and Tony work at the steelworks, and hopefully we can get Geordie in as well."

Tony didn't have a clue about steel, lucky for me I had worked at one in Gateshead before I joined the army. The drinks started to flow and David started to relax with us. Tony got out his camera, "Let's have some photos lads." He called out to Shannon, "Can you take them please?"

She walked over and Tony got us up against the back wall, just where the painting was, making sure it was in the photo. The night went well, and David was relaxed. Tony and Glenn had headed for the bar to get the next round, and while they were gone I asked David about the painting.

"Why was it that Rob didn't want to speak about it?"

"You don't want to know."

"Why not?" I asked.

"They've got him to paint quite a few, and he doesn't like doing them, he thinks something's going on, but doesn't know what, they're quite particular in what they want in them. This one on the wall, for instance, see the blood tear drops …?" David was starting to get carried away with the story he was telling me, but when Tony and Glenn came back to the table he stopped in his tracks as if he had been caught doing something wrong. He looked back at me and said "I can't tell you, I'll be in so much trouble."

"Off who?" I asked.

"The doormen. They told Rob he wasn't to speak about them to anyone, not even me."

"OK," I said, "leave it. I don't want you in trouble mate."

The mood had changed, it seemed to have gone quiet with a cold feeling at the table. I changed the topic and asked David about his singing, how he'd got into it.

"My dad was a good singer, he travelled the clubs up north singing with a group he put together, and he got me into it."

"I would love to do that," I said. "Me and Tony have a mess about singing to the radio."

"Why don't you come down on Friday night? We have a go as you please on."

Tony piped up "Am up for that mate, we'll be here."

I didn't get a chance to speak. I was going to say the same, as it would get us in with him and Rob. By this time we'd had quite a lot to drink and Glenn said it was time to go. "Me and Tony have an early start in the morning, and with a bit luck so will Geordie next week." I'd forgotten they'd said about them working at the steelworks. We stood up, drank the rest of the pints, and said goodnight to David and the lasses behind the bar. We then headed for the taxi rank at the station, and got back to camp at about 23:45hours. We decided to head straight to our rooms and get our heads down.

The next day we joined the rest of the lads on parade, reported to the garage as normal, and at 10:00 hours NAFFI break I headed up to see BSM Bob. I gave him the low-down on what we got the previous night and he instructed me to go about my normal job and inform the rest of the lads to do the same. This was it for the next two or three days, BSM Bob had it sorted for the three of us to have the Friday night off so we could go to Good Brewers and try and get more information on the paintings; in the meantime BSM Bob had got the regiment photographer to develop the photos Tony had got taken by the young lass in the bar. It had been decided that me, Tony and Glenn would go to the pub as arranged to have a drink with Dave and hopefully his mate that owned the nightclubs – his name we hadn't been told yet. The rest of the lads would be in the area looking out for us.

On the Friday we all got on parade at about 16:30 hours, this was the norm, the weekend was here and every Friday all the batteries would do the same. The Battery BC would give his chat, *well done lads you have worked hard, now have a good weekend and keep out of trouble,* and the same as every week Dunc would say softly *up yours, sir,* and it always set the lads off giggling, trying their best not to upset the BC or he would stop us all from going out of camp. This time we held it together and got out. It was agreed me, Tony and Glenn would head to town together, the rest of the lads would make their own way to town and meet up there.

I headed for the cookhouse for tea – Fish Friday; there were always four or five choices but fish and chips was always the one I had. I don't know why because my Friday tea at home was always liver. When I headed back to my block, Evo caught me up. I didn't find out for some years that his real name was Andy Evans, he'd always been known as Evo.

Brit, Evo and myself served in the Falklands together in the same sub, we had some good times together and that was where I really got to know them both properly. Evo was as mad as a hatter. I remember one time, it was just after the war had finished, our sub was down in the valley of San Carlos Bay, 21 Delta Raper site. Our job was to look after the ships if Argentina tried to have another go. The day was quiet, so me and Evo decided to head to the beach to see what we could scrounge. The stuff that was lying on the beach was no one's business. I found a 84mm live shell. We thought it would be fun to see if we could get it to go off by throwing it up in the air and seeing if it would land on its firing pin – stupid I know, but that was what we were like back then. As we were heading back to the sub, Evo decided he wanted to have a farm.

"Are you from a farming background mate?" I asked.

"No, don't be daft, not when I get out of the army, I mean *now.*"

"And what are you going to have in it, and how are you going to keep them, stupid?" I said.

"I have it all worked out, you'll see."

He never got the farm, but we all had a great time watching him try, he was definitely one of the lads.

"So Geordie, what is it *you're* up to?" I knew exactly what he was on about but couldn't say a word.

"Don't know what you're on about mate."

"Don't give me that shit, something's going on and I *will* find out!" He was a lot like Donny, he picked up on things and worked things out without having a clue from the start. I had to speak with BSM Bob on Monday about him; he had to join us because he wouldn't give up until he found out what it was we were up to. I changed the subject and as we got to the block I headed off to my room. "See you in town later mate, if you're going?" For a minute I forgot I was meeting Glenn and Tony, lucky for me he had decided to head home for the weekend.

After I had showered and dressed, I went outside to sit in the last of the sunshine, have a bottle of broon and a smoke. All was quiet, the sun was still warm on my face, and the birds were singing in the trees, times like this I had started to enjoy after what we had been through. I felt happy and safe somehow. Why, I didn't know, but I wasn't bothered, it felt good and I was enjoying it. Just as all was quiet Dunc decided to spoil it. "Hee Geordie, give us a tab mate." I handed him the packet and lighter and he sat next to me.

"What is this shit you were going to tell me the other day?"

"What was that mate?" I said, not remembering what he was on about.

"The shit about you being bullied back home, is it true mate?"

SHIT! I didn't want to get into it, but I knew Dunc, he wouldn't leave it until I spoke about it.

"Yes mate, it's true I had a bit of a hard time when I was younger."

"Don't believe you, you're full of shit."

"No, it's true mate, it all started when I was about eight, it would start after a game of football in the street next to my house, we would play what we called 'gates'. My gate would be one goal, and over the road the Drummands' gate would be the other. If the ball belonged to one of the lads l would have to take it to his house when we had finished the game when the rest of them would go off doing something else."

"Did you not tell him to shove it?"

"I tried it once, I threw the ball down the street and told him to take it himself, but he ran after me and I got a kicking for it. That was when it started to get worse, the word got to school, and the fighting started. Some of the lads would get other lads to set about me."

"What do you mean *get other lads to set about you?*"

"It was more fun for them to watch me getting a kicking than them doing it themselves."

"Didn't you fight back?"

"Yes, at first, but then there would be another one waiting in the wings to jump me, so it became easier to have one kicking instead of loads."

"Was it the hard lads that would give you the kickings?"

"No, they just had the entertainment, but put the odd boot in. I couldn't speak about it to anyone, if my dad found out that would be worse, he always got me and my brother to fight with him … to him he was trying to harden us up, but for me I didn't want to hit him. My mam would tell him to leave me, but I was a big soft puff to him. I don't think he meant it but I didn't do anything for him to be proud of me." For some reason I was starting to pour my heart out to Dunc; I think this was the first time I had ever spoken about the bullying, except for one lad I could speak to about anything – my good mate Dave McGlen. He knew what I had been through, he tried to help me on many occasions, but I didn't want him being dragged into it, so I tried to keep him out of it.

"When it really got bad was when I started the high school. I was then forced to take money to school for them. My dad would have killed me if he ever found out what I had started to do. He had a ten gallon whisky bottle he saved his change in, and when my brother went to sleep, I would sneak into Mam and Dad's room and take some of the change from the bottle. That was until I got caught one night by my mam and sister Val. That was a lot worse than any kicking I had ever had, the shame I felt stayed with me for years. I never did get to say sorry to Mam, *or* my sister, for what I had let myself get into. Taking a kicking was the easy part, having to pinch and lie to my family was lower than low."

On the next Sunday afternoon we had a game of football on the old airfield. At about 16:00 hours we decided to head back to the block to get cleaned up and head down town for a few drinks; before this we all got our uniforms ready for parade the next day. This was normal for most of the lads, as if you had a good drink on the Sunday you were never in a state to bull your boots or press your uniform on the

Monday morning. So me, Tony, Brit and Dunc jumped in a taxi and headed to Scunthorpe, it's one of the squaddies' local drinking areas, and there was always a lot of lassies there if you fancied picking one up. We had a good night, nothing out of the ordinary, we met a few of the lads from the regiment and stayed with them until we headed back.

When we got to the block there was a lad sitting on a suitcase outside my room. He stood up and asked if one of us was Gunner Gordon.

"Yes, me, why do you ask?"

"My name is Chris McVeigh and I have been informed I am to share your room."

"So why haven't you gone in?"

"The lad down the corridor said you would drop me if I went in."

"Don't be daft, they're pulling your leg."

Brit piped up, "I'll drop you just for the fun of it!"

The poor lad was shitting it.

"Fuck off, Brit, let the lad alone," I said, and opened the door to my room. "Go on, Chris, get yourself in."

Dunc stepped forward and grabbed Chris by his hair.

"… and *I* will sort you tomorrow good and proper."

Brit and Dunc laughed. I pushed him off and picked up Chris's case and pushed him into the room, the lad was shitting it. When I shut the door, Brit was shouting "*YOU'RE DEAD BOY*". I could hear them laughing as they walked away to their room.

I popped the kettle on. "That's yours," I said, and pointed to the bed on the left of the room. I then got two cups out of my locker. "You will need to start and give me some cash every week for the brew kit mate," I said.

"Yes, no problem Gunner Gordon."

"No Chris, Geordie is my name, well, it's what I'm known as in the army. The two lads you met are Brit and Dunc, and don't take any notice of them, they just like to see the new lads shit it a bit." As the kettle was starting to boil I opened a locker. "You can have this locker Chris." I took some of my civilian clothing out and dropped on my bed. We chatted for a while and he asked if he could smoke in the room.

"No, I don't allow it in my room, but if you wish to smoke in a room, you can swap with one of the lads that don't smoke."

"No, it's fine Geordie, I'll just go outside when I fancy one."

"Come on, I'll go with you." I could see he was a bit concerned about going out on his own, as he might bump into Brit or Dunc. As we headed out we saw Tony walking along the road with Glenn and Kenny.

"Hi Geordie, who's this, your new bum chum?" Glenn called out.

"This is Chris, he's sharing a room with me."

They all shook his hand, "Welcome to the regiment Chris."

I could see the look on his face change from fear to relief, until Glenn said, "You'll have a good time here, if you fit in … if not, it will be hell for you."

"That's right, frighten the shit out of the lad," I said.

"You'll be fine," Tony said. He and Glenn then went back to their rooms, and Kenny headed to his block after saying goodnight.

Chris and I sat on one of the park type benches in front of the block, the sky was clear and the moon shone over the top of the NAFFI clear and bight. I got up off the seat, and told Chris to stay where he was. I headed back to my room, went into the top drawer of the set at the side of my bed, got out two hamlet cigars, two glasses and a bottle of scotch whisky. I headed back outside and sat next to Chris, handed him a glass and cigar, and we sat there just chatting about nothing much. The next time I looked at my watch it was 03:25 hours. "*SHIT* we should get our heads down mate, you have a big day tomorrow, getting to know the lads and the bosses." He seemed to be a good lad, not had a lot in his life, but I had a feeling that was going to change, as I felt he would be good for the group, though I would have to get to know him a lot more before I could really decide.

The next morning I was up with the larks, off for my run, and on my return hit the kettle switch, and headed off for a shower. When I returned, the cups had been put next to the kettle, and Chris was sat on his bed. "I thought I would make the tea, is that OK Geordie?"

"Yes, mate. I could get used to this, having my morning brew made for me." He looked as if he had set himself up for a job he would have to stick to for ever. It was not the case, he turned out to be like Dunc, a lazy git, not one for the morning. It turned out that I would make it every day for the rest of the time we shared the room.

Chris settled in well with the lads and, to my surprise, Dunc and Brit tucked him under their wing and they all hit it off well together.

The days after just seemed to be the same as normal, up for a run, off to breakfast, on parade, and given the jobs for the day, the odd guard duty, nights in the gym doing my training, weekends on the piss with the lads – we all still would keep an eye on Good Brewers for the doormen, just in case they gave anything away, but nothing.

One day I was sat in my room trying to write a letter home to my mate Dave. When I say *try*, I mean it. Writing was the hardest thing for me, but I still didn't ask for help off the lads. They all knew I struggled with spelling but I couldn't bring myself to ask for help. One good thing was that after every letter I wrote to Dave, he would send a letter back – but never as you would expect. On the bottom would be my spellings that were wrong, and next to them would be the right spellings. I started to make a list. It was hard, as I would find it hard to read them, it was easier to read my own spellings. So I started to write them my way and next to it would be the right way. Dave probably didn't realise but he helped me a lot. I also got the same from my sister Val. The hard part was keeping it up. If I was writing letters to them on a regular basis I started to get better, but as soon as I went a week or so without writing, I would lose it, and would have to start again from scratch. For some reason I just couldn't remember how to spell.

Just as I was finishing the letter, one of the T battery lads knocked on the door. *"Come in"* I called out. Chris was out with Brit and Dunc. The door opened and the lad there was one I knew well. "Geordie, you have to go to your battery office now."

"What for?" I asked.

"I don't know, but I've been told to get you to get seven more." – Tony, Glenn, Donny, Dunc, Brit and one from 9 battery, Kenny. *SHIT!* something's going down. I could feel the adrenaline pumping through my body, I got a flashback to the shed, sweat balls covered my forehead. I didn't know if I was excited or scared. The lad asked if I was OK, as I had gone white in the face. "Yes, fine mate," I said. "You had better go and inform Glenn and Tony, and get Kenny from the 9 battery block and I'll get the rest of the lads." I informed him that Brit and Dunc were down town and I would inform the BSM. I assumed it was him we had to report to. The lad left my room and headed down the corridor to Tony's room. I got my shoes on and left my room. As I turned to lock the door, I saw Tony and Glenn heading up the corridor. "This is it," Glenn said. I could see the excitement on Glenn's face, he was well up for it, whatever *it* was.

When we got to the hangar Donny and Kenny had got there ahead of us. We all then headed to the office block. We walked into the BSM's office and there were the two officers from the SAS sat at the BSM's desk; it was the two we had met after the wilderness hunt. BSM Bob was sat on the window sill, the chairs had been set out for use. We were all on a high as we had been waiting for this for some time.

"Dunc and Brit are down town, sir," Tony said.

"OK lads, two of you can go down and get them after we have spoken with you. Right, there is something going down, we need you ready to go in three hours. You will have two Land Rovers and two radio cars, you will tell *nobody* about this." BSM Bob looked at me. "Do you think Chris and Evo are ready for this?" Before I had a chance to answer Donny piped up, "Yes, sir, definitely. I have been watching them closely for weeks, sir, and they are ready."

"OK, get them ready to move and say nothing until you're on route." One of the SAS officers handed Tony an envelope and instructed him to head south on the A1, stop at the first service station, and then open the envelope.

"Right lads, we're relying on you. You will be met at about 03:00 hours, all your instructions are in the envelope."

Tony and Donny had been instructed they were in charge, and we had to follow all instructions to the letter. Any questions? Nothing. We all just sat, not really believing what was happening; we all had waited for this for so long, but now it was here we couldn't get our heads around it. This was real and we were the team that had been picked to do the job. Someone, somewhere, had faith in us, and we would have to deliver. For me personally, I was more than ready. I wanted to put a stop to all of this shit, and make them that had set it all up pay.

We all set off to our rooms. I was ready to move straight away, my kit was always packed ready to go. I also had Chris doing the same. It made sense, the more you were ready, the less stressful it was when the time came to move.

Tony got me to get one of the cars and head down town with Glenn to look for Dunc, Brit and Chris, while he headed to the NAFFI for Jock and Platty. It wouldn't be hard, they always drank in the same place, and if they weren't there the barmaid would know where they would have headed.

As we pulled up outside the pub they had just walked out the door to head off to the next bar. Glenn called out to them, Brit looked over. Without saying a word he knew. "Get in the car," he then said to Dunc and Chris. Chris was the one that was taken aback by it all but did as Brit said. As I pulled away, Dunc asked, "Is this it lads?"

"Yes," I said. Nothing else was said all the way back to camp.

When I pulled up outside the block, I told Chris to get in the room and pick up all his quick action deployment gear, get his combats on – and *no* questions. Chris didn't have a clue what was going on, but he did as I said. Before long he'd headed back out to the car, dropped his kit in the boot and jumped in the back seat. Donny had already got Evo packed and ready; Donny, Evo and Tony had the two Land Rovers and the other car outside the block ready. When Dunc and Brit came running out with their kit and started to clamber into the cars, one of the other lads came out asking what was going on. Tony told him we had been given an exercise, and if we completed it, Geordie and Dunc would be going for promotion. At that he jumped in the Land Rover and set off, headed down to the Scunthorpe road and along the M62 towards the A1.

It took about 1½ hours to reach the services, and as we pulled in we all felt apprehensive, not knowing what we were driving into. Donny was leading the convoy in one of the Land Rovers. He stopped at the far corner of one of the car parks away from any other cars, and we all pulled in alongside him. There we sat. No one made a move to get out, none of us knew what to expect; did we have to meet someone? Or was it just to read the instructions Tony had been given? As we'd driven in we all seemed to be looking around, what for we didn't know but all seemed to be as it should be. There were people moving from cars to and from the services and nothing seemed out of place or suspicious.

Dunc was the first to make a move. He climbed out the car and headed to Tony's Land Rover, opened the driver's door, and held his hand out as if to say give me the letter. Tony looked at him knowing he had to do it himself. As he took it out of his pocket he looked at Dunc. "No mate, I've got this." As he opened the envelope, there was silence, you could feel the tension. This was not just a letter, but something that was going to change the life of us all; from this point on we weren't just soldiers, we had stepped into a role that would affect us for the rest of our lives. Yes, we had been to hell and back when me, Brit and Kenny had been taken off to the Yorkshire moors, but this felt *real*. I don't know about the rest – would it just be me, Kenny and Brit that felt this way, as we had been on the receiving end of the kickings in the moors? The rest of the lads had probably done this before, to save our lives on the moors, although Chris and Evo hadn't done anything like this before, this to them was new. I could see they both had the look of horror on their faces when Glenn gave them the story of what had happened to me Brit and Kenny. I knew questions would be coming my way from the two of them, first from Chris – we shared a room and I hadn't let on – but Evo I think would understand why we couldn't say a word.

Tony was fumbling with the paper as he took it out of the envelope. There were two pieces, and as he unfolded them I could see there were page numbers in the top right corner. As he read, he got Dunc to wave the rest of us over. He had to send two of us to the restaurant in the services; we were to sit at the table in the far corner by the last window; we would be joined by two men dressed in blue jeans and black jumpers, and they would bring us drinks as if we had walked in together and were just keeping the table for us all. Tony decided to send Glenn and myself, the rest had to stay put.

As we walked across the car park I could feel the tension in my body, Glenn was probably feeling the same. We never said a word to each other, just slowly walked and looked around as we went. Nothing out of the ordinary, people going to their cars and into the services, no one out of place, no one looking suspicious, not even a group of young lads messing around seemed to draw a lot of attention to themselves. It wasn't until we stepped into the restaurant, I could feel the sweat running down my spine and the shirt sticking to my body. Glenn looked at me and I sensed he knew how I was feeling. "You OK mate?" he said. "Yes, just a bit apprehensive."

I knew I had to do this, I *wanted* to do this, but I couldn't help feeling I wasn't the violent type. However, I had to look at it not as violence but revenge ... revenge for myself and everyone that had been through the same, and some that hadn't come home after it. We had to do this for the families of them all. As we looked over to the table we saw there were two office type men sat there. I walked over to the table behind them, looked at them and could see they had finished their all day breakfast and would be ready to leave soon. As predicted, after about five minutes they got up and headed out. Glenn and myself got straight up and sat in their seats (anyone seeing us do this would think we were like two schoolkids running to get the back seat on the upstairs of the school bus).

We both sat facing the restaurant with our backs to the wall, we didn't have a clue how long we would be there, but for some reason we kept looking at our watches. It was a very tense time for us both; we kept looking at people coming in and heading towards us, one after another we were disappointed as they peeled off to tables in front of us. Then they came. One was big, 6ft plus, and the other was about 5ft 6, not of a big build, and not one you would think to be in the army, let alone on any type of major task like we were. They both carried a tray with two full English breakfasts and two cups of tea. When they sat down, I could see Glenn getting ready to speak. I was thinking they would be the ones to start the conversation, but no, Glenn said straight out and in a confident voice, "Hi lads which one's mine?"

They both looked at him, then smiled. "This is yours mate," and handed over the tray. "Get stuck in lads." The one sat facing me said, without looking up from his plate, "I'm Dave, and this is Tommy, we know who you are so don't say a word, Geordie and Glenn." They had obviously done their homework. Meanwhile, back at the cars, Tony had opened the second bit of paper and was reading it out to the lads.

The group was to be split into two teams, one group would go off with Dave and the other with Tommy, but who would go with who was down to me and Glenn. Dave informed us he was to take one group to Dartmoor, and we would be training in survival and ambush tactics, the other was to go with Tommy, for unarmed combat, observation and infiltration. It was a no brainer, me Glenn and Tony all had unarmed combat training, Kenny and Brit were the same, so that left Donny, Dunc, Evo, Chris, Jock and Platty, that way no matter what the groups would be we would have one of each in them.

"Stop there," I said, "we haven't got a clue who you are, so how can we trust you?" Dave asked me to go to the toilets and he would follow. As I headed in I could see two men stood just by the gift shop. I thought it was a bit strange as although they seemed to be together, they seemed to be avoiding one another. As I stepped into the toilet they followed. I was standing as if I was having a slash, and they came and stood either side of me; this was not looking good for me. I hadn't pulled down my zip, I could sense the atmosphere growing tense. I was feeling the distance between them and was working out my moves to put them down, when one of them said, "Geordie, you need to relax mate, we have followed you from your camp all the way here … when you go out, go to the window overlooking the car park, you will see two blue cars to the left of your mates." I turned and headed out. I could feel them following close behind, I felt uneasy as I walked. When I got to the window, I looked over to Tony and the lads, and just as the men had said there were two blue cars, inside were three men in each. I turned to look back into the restaurant. The two men had followed, they were stood behind me. "Don't panic mate," one said, "this is all part of the training, this is just to let you all know, what you're going into is nothing like your normal army training, you have to be vigilant at all times … keep looking."

I hadn't noticed Glenn outside with Dave and Tommy. The six men got out of the cars and headed over to Tony and the lads – they looked like any other group of men walking away from their cars, until they surrounded the cars and Land Rovers. Neither Tony nor any of the lads had seen them coming, except Donny and Evo. They had seen them but didn't suspect anything, until it was too late. The six men had split and run straight at the lads. Dunc and Brit were lying on the grass, Tony, Jock and Platty were sat in one of the cars, Donny and Evo were stood by one of the Land Rovers, it was too late for them to do anything. The men stopped, turned and ran at them. One went to Brit and Dunc and just stood looking at them; two ran at Donny and Evo, the other three hit the car. The lads couldn't believe what had just happened, no one was expecting this at all, but it was a good lesson we had all learnt: *always be alert and never let your guard down.*

The two men with me turned and said, "You parked over in the corner to keep away from trouble, but none of your mates were alert. You always be observant no matter where you are." We headed outside to Glenn and then we all walked over to the cars. Dave and his mates had a laugh at me and my mates' expense, but to be fair we should've been on the ball, we knew we had to meet people here and still didn't know what we had been sent into. Tommy got us all together and informed us what was happening. We then split into our teams and headed off with the training teams, me and my lot headed to Dartmoor with one of the cars and a Land Rover. The rest headed to Hereford to do classroom training to start with.

As we set off you could sense the excitement among us, this was certainly different to the normal stuff we did. I started to feel I was someone, someone that had started with nothing, a lad from a council estate, left school unable to read or write, was bullied until I was 18, and now I had learned to read and write a lot better, not perfect by any means, but I had help. All of the lads knew about it and helped, they never took the piss. Yes, they had a laugh at the spellings, but they *helped*. As for the bullying, that had gone, I had learned to fight back and now could handle myself. I wouldn't say I was hard but I had learned to defend myself, I felt I had become something, something important, I had a meaning in life, and had a job to do that meant something to me. As we drove along the A1 onto the M1 I looked at the men that had come in the car with us. There was a feeling of confidence about them, you could sense the pride they had being in the best fighting force in the world, and they were about to train with tactics most people could only dream about. In the car was Dave, Brit, Glenn and myself, and in the Land Rover was Tony, Kenny and three of the SAS lads that I hadn't got their names yet. As we drove, Dave was giving us hints of what we would be doing for the next week.

Back at camp BSM Bob Wilson had got the battery on parade, the RSM had informed him that people had started to ask questions about our whereabouts and that something was going on that no one had answers to. The story was simple: because of the Falklands war the SAS required more training, as the landing of the special forces had not gone to plan, and people lost lives unnecessarily, so we had been chosen to act as enemy for an exercise they had put together. BSM Bob still was asked a lot more questions, but he had answers for them. Why us, who, how many, and why Kenny Dinsdale, as he was from a different battery? The answer to the last question was probably the easiest to give: Kenny had always wanted to join the SAS and BSM Denis Welsh had asked if he could be part of it to give him an insight to it all – that everyone could believe as you always saw him running with a pack on his back, saliva dripping from his mouth, and at times tears running down his face from the pain he would put himself through. That seemed to stop the questions and the mood in the camp changed – from questions to laughter – as we all knew training with the SAS was never fun or without pain.

Donny and the rest of the lads had headed to Hereford for self defence training, deploying tactics and body language observation. It all seems straightforward but believe me there is a lot more than just looking at someone. Donny and Dunc seemed to take charge of the lads with them and rightly so, as they both had a good understanding of what was going on.

We had been travelling for about two hours when Dave instructed Glenn to turn off the M1 at the next exit. Dave continued to give him instructions for the next 20 minutes or so. He obviously knew the area as he had no map, and was giving the instructions well in advance. We turned in to a wood and drove up a track for about 1200 yards, then stopped. Dave got us all out of the car and Land Rover, and set off on foot, at a pace we struggled to keep up with. In the distance I could see a 4-tonne truck and five men; this wasn't Dartmoor and this wasn't what we had expected, so what was going on? All was to be revealed when we got to the truck – it was full of all kinds of equipment that we would need, things we didn't have a clue about, but would be essential.

I looked at Glenn and his face lit up like a kid at Christmas; he knew *exactly* what this lot was, and had dreamed about them for years, but this kit you couldn't get on the open market, or from your regiment. We all sat in a row while Dave and his lads introduced us to them all, some of the survival equipment was out of this world. Once Dave finished we had to take what we thought we would need for one week, pack our Bergens and head to the edge of the wood. As we sat wondering what was going on, Tony told us to be quiet … we could hear the sound of a chopper in the distance.

Brit looked at me. "Is that what I think it is mate?" he said.

"Yes, it's a Chinook." The sound of it was different to any other helicopter; we all called it a *wocker wocker* because of the sound it made with the double rotor blades. As it approached Dave got us ready to board. There was nothing we hadn't already been shown with this, as we had practised this time and time again and the equipment we used was *rapper* which we often had to deploy in some remote areas – so helly landing was easier than trying to drive in with it.

It seemed we had only been on the chopper about twenty minutes before we got the signal to prepare to DEBUS. As I grabbed my Bergen the tailgate started to lower. Dave and his lads stood next to it, strapped in by lines hanging from the roof of the chopper. Just as we got up and ready to move, Dave gave us the signal to sit back down. What was going on? Something had happened. Dave was chatting on the net with the pilot, the chopper banked to the right and seemed to dive, this put my heart in my mouth. Looking at the rest of the lads I could see they had the same feeling by the look on their faces, this wasn't right, something was wrong. I looked at Dave, he gave me the thumbs up, as if to say *it's OK*, but that didn't make me feel any better. The chopper was still dropping, but it seemed now to be under control. We flew low for some time, then Dave switched the headsets on so we all could hear what was going on.

"A change of plan lads, all is OK but we have been given new instructions."

What had changed? Maybe Dave and his lads had to be deployed in an SAS job and we would be dropped off and have to make our own way back to camp. The chopper started to hover over a grass field. Brit looked out of the small window next to him, he looked over to me and pointed down towards the ground. I looked down and saw at the side of the field there were three cars and three men stood by them. Again, Dave got us ready to DEBUS, and this time we did. We ran straight out the back and got in a group and sat waiting for the chopper to take off. Dave and his lads stayed on the chopper and off it went.

Tony and Glenn looked at me. Brit called out, "LOOK LADS!" The three men from the cars had started to come over towards us. We got up and started heading towards them, one called out, "Which one of you is Geordie Gordon?" "That's me," I said. "Pick one of your lads and come with us, the rest of you head to that wood and stay there," and he pointed to the woods to the left of us.

We were in the countryside somewhere, but where we didn't have a clue. They introduced themselves and informed me the situation with the doormen had changed. "What do you mean?" Tony wanted to know.

"Big Bob has been located."

My heart sank. *Shit*, they've found him and we're off the job, but no, the rest of his fucked up disciples have started to talk, they're still held at Hereford. Them that had been captured in the Yorkshire moors were still held; the ones that had been killed, had been sent to the military morgue, so at the moment, as far as the public and their families were concerned, they're all still missing. We'd been informed that Big Bob was in Wales, Haverfordwest area, lucky for us, BSM Bob was from that area, but the trouble for us was to get him back on board. He had dropped out to work from camp only. As he had a young family, he had decided to keep out of the action end of things, but now we needed him, back out in the field as we call it.

The three men handed the car keys over and informed us there were cards in the glove compartment for Jacksons clothing store, and a credit card. We had an unlimited amount to spend on clothes and equipment – we would need a lot of civilian clothes, and we would have to pay for digs. They asked if we understood all we had been informed of, and then they headed off to the wood where my lads had been sent. As they ran into the wood, Brit headed towards them. The rest came out, they stopped and chatted with the three men. As Brit and the lads headed over towards us, we could hear the chopper coming back over the woods … down it came and off the SAS lads went into the distance. As the sound of the chopper started to fade, silence grew, not even the sound of birds could be heard. It sent a shiver down my spine. We were in this for real again, but now I felt stronger, tougher and really ready for it. Things had changed. I didn't know what, but I felt good about myself again.

Tony and Glenn took control and split us between the three cars. Tony and Brit took the front car, me and Kenny in the second, and Glenn in the back one on his own. We headed off until we hit Bristol, where we stopped at a service station and headed for the cafe for an all day breakfast. Kenny started the chat. He thought we should contact BSM Bob to give him the situation we had ended up in. Tony thought we should contact BSM Ian Tate to convince Bob to join us. Ian was good friends with him, so if anyone could talk him around he could.

As we were all in combats we headed to the high street to

get some civilian clothes. As we walked, people looked at us, Bristol wasn't the place you would normally see squaddies. It was a cool windy day, a little overcast, but dry. After we got back to the cars we headed for the M50, stopped at the first lay-by we came to, took turns to head down the side embankment to change into civilian clothes, and packed all combats into one car boot. This meant if we had to get into them we had only to ensure that we had that car with us at all times. I had a map I picked up at the services and had a good look through it. There was a small fishing village Milford Haven about twenty minutes outside of the town, and we headed straight for it to look for a B&B. The time was now getting on and we would have to contact Ian soon as he would be heading home for the day, but to be fair, it wouldn't matter as we had nothing worked out as yet, so we just had to keep our heads down, keep out of trouble until we could sort out tactics. None of us had given a thought to Platty and the rest of the lads. Then Brit asked the question, "Is Platty and the lads going to join us?" This we didn't have a clue, but we could ask Ian if he knew anything about this, if anybody knew *he* would, as it was him that got us the back up from the SAS when we had been taken to the Yorkshire moors to be hunted as live bait.

As we drove through Milford Haven, the roads seemed to be a lot quieter than we had all thought, but to be fair we all came from the big cities, Newcastle, London, Burnley, apart from Donny – he belonged to the lakes, quiet in the winter, but in the summer the place would be full of visitors from abroad. For some reason everyone seemed to love the lakes, but Donny wasn't with us yet, and we didn't even know if he or the rest of the lads would be joining us.

As we drove towards a small village called Johnston, we noticed a small petrol station on the right just past a small row of shops. We drove in and lined up the cars behind one another at the first pump. Me, Kenny and Brit stayed in the cars and tried to keep out of sight; if Big Bob was in the area we didn't want him to see us. The rest of the lads would be fine, but us three he had seen and would definitely recognise. Tony and Glenn headed towards the kiosk to ask the old lady that stood behind the counter if she knew of any good B&Bs she could recommend for us. As they headed in, an old man appeared at the doorway.

"You need the cars filled up boys?" he said in the strongest Welsh accent I had ever heard.

"Yes please, sir," Glenn said. Tony then said "We're all together mate, so I'm paying for the three cars."

"That's not a problem boy," the old man said, as he headed over to the cars, and started with the front one. He took off the filler cap and started to fill them up. As he looked down the line of the three cars, he pointed to each car in turn, indicating for the cars to be moved forward to the pump. Tony and Glenn grabbed a few bits off the display counter and took them to the old lady. "I'd like to pay for these and the petrol for the three cars please," Tony said, looking at her.

"That's not a problem boy," she said as she started ringing the items through the till. The till was a big old fashioned one, the sort you had to put all your strength into just to push one button. Her fingers had to be so strong. Glenn felt a bit sorry for her, as she repeated the process for each item. "That will be £17 boy," she said as she started putting the items into a bag she had pulled from behind the counter.

That seems a lot Tony thought, as he looked at Glenn. The old lady noticed and said that was for the petrol as well. Tony looked out of the window and saw the old man had finished filling the cars, and was now checking the oil. This never happened in the cities, but he supposed out here there wasn't a lot of traffic, so they would have time to give a little more as a good gesture.

Tony asked if there were any good B&Bs in the area. "Not many boy," she replied. "How many is it for boy?"

"Six at the moment, but there could be another six in a day or two," Tony replied.

"You boys on holiday or just a lads weekend away?"

"No, we're looking to be settling down here for a while, if we can find work," Glenn piped up.

"Well, you could just be lucky boys, I have three homes I rent out as holiday homes, and they just happen to be empty at the moment, but you would only be able to have them for two months, as they are booked after that. Did you say there is twelve of you's?"

"Yes," Tony said. "Are they far away from here?"

"No boy, just around the corner. It's a quiet street so you would have to behave yourselves as the rest of the street is full of old people."

She had to be in her late 70s herself, so the street residents had to be *very* old, but this could be a good thing, as long as we kept our heads down and the noise down we should be OK, Tony thought.

The old lady opened a drawer under the counter and pulled out three sets of keys, put out her hand, and said, "Sorry boys but I need cash up front for two weeks, it is £10 a week for each house."

"No problem Miss," Glenn said, as he pulled out a handful of notes and handed the lady £40. "If we need them longer, can we pay one week ahead each week please?"

"Yes, not a problem boys, but £40 for three for two weeks wasn't £40 when I went to school."

Tony looked at Glenn. "Come on Glenn," he said, "don't try and rob the lady." They laughed and apologised as Glenn handed over the other £20.

"Don't worry boys, I may be old but I'm not daft," she chuckled, as she dropped the keys into Tony's hand. "Now you tell Bill to come in and I'll get him to take you there." She pointed to Tony and off he went. Tony and Glenn both smiled, as they thought she was so sweet, but the boss of Bill and anyone that she came across.

Glenn and Tony headed back to the cars. Bill was still checking the oil on the last car, as Tony approached and handed him the keys. "Your good lady said you have to take us to your homes you rent out."

"Oh, did she now?" he said as he looked back at the kiosk. The old lady stood in the window looking out. She reminded me of my Grandma Gordon.

If Grandma Gordon ever told you to do something, she had a look that said *do it and don't ask questions.* I loved to visit her, it was mostly on a Sunday. My dad would drop my sisters, brother and me off, pop in for about ten minutes before he would head off to the bar for his Sunday afternoon drinking. Grandma always baked on a Sunday, so we would all have a bit more to eat than normal, with there being nine of us.

Mam did what she could with the money she had, we always got fed. It may not have been a lot, but she looked after us all, and we all got the same. That was until we started work. We then got what I called an *adult meal*, a big plate, a normal dinner plate. I still remember getting my first big meal – liver, onion and chips – the best. I also remember my first pay packet, £24, that was double what my mates got. Dave McGlen was a motorcycle mechanic at Harry Woods for £11 a week, and that was about the same as the rest of the lads, so £24 for me was massive. When I took my first pay home, and Mam asked if I wanted to give her all of my pay and she would give me pocket money, and still pay for my clothes, I thought *I don't think so.* Or I could give her board money, she suggested. Board, I thought, that would be better for me. The good thing was she said it was up to me how much I paid. I thought about it for a little while. Would £10 be OK? Yes, that would be fine, she said. Great, that meant I would have £14 for myself, that was more than Dave was getting before he gave his mam her board. Little did I know my sisters had only been giving Mam £5! Gutted at the time, when I found out, but I was glad I gave her it, because she did have it hard, and did all she could for us.

As Bill headed to his wife, we all got back into the cars. Tony was in the front car. We thought Bill would either get in with Tony or in his own car, but no, he went to a shed at the side of the garage, and got out an old butcher's bike. We all couldn't stop laughing, so funny three cars following a peddle bike along a road. It was about two miles from the garage to where we would be staying. Eventually we turned right into a small cul-de-sac with about 25 houses on the street. And apart from one small cut through between two of the houses, the way we came in was the only other way out. There was a block of five houses at the far end of the cul-de-sac, three of them were for us, all three houses joined together. One was on the end of the block; between the other two was an arch that ran from the front through to the back gardens; there were two gates separating them. As I sat in the car looking out at the houses, I was thinking how we would sort out who was going to stay in which house and that we could turn one of the bedrooms into an ops room – that would have to be in the middle house so the noise from the radios wouldn't travel through the walls into the other residents' houses. We would also have any meetings in the same house to keep the noise level down. As we started to get out of the cars, old Bill shouted out to an old man in the garden across the street.

"Good day, Dave, you sorting through the weeds boy?"

"Yes Bill, I did yours this morning."

"Great boy, I'll pay you at the end of the month as normal."

"No worries boy," and he picked up his spade and drove it into the ground.

We followed Bill into the end house. He informed us that it had four bedrooms, and the other two only had three. That was spot on for us; we would put six lads in the end house, two in the middle one, and four in the last house, but that wouldn't be up to me, though it would make sense. We would need radio equipment, weapons, clothing, food, cooking equipment, and more, so storing it all in one place and the middle house would make sense, but let's see what the lads thought.

When Bill left us, we all checked out the houses. Tony got us all together in the middle house and asked us our thoughts. I put mine to the lads, and it was yes from them all. I think that was the first time we had all agreed on an idea. Glenn came up with who would be in each room, but we didn't know if the rest of the lads would be joining us. Brit said we should contact camp and speak with BSM Bob, he would have been in contact with Hereford. So that's what we did. Kenny and Brit headed off to look for a phone box, while the rest of us emptied the cars and put everything into the living room of the middle house until we knew who was going to live where. While we were doing so, Glenn remembered we had been sent here to dig out Big Bob, the shit of a doorman, and he knew Kenny and Brit. We didn't have a clue if he was living in the area we had settled in, so it was a big risk letting Brit and Kenny out there. Too late to do anything about it now, so all we could do was wait and hope they didn't get seen. Luck for them, they found a phone box at bottom of the estate down by the harbour. It was only two streets away from the houses we had, through a cut at the side of the cul-de-sac, that also gave them the chance to suss out the second exit if it was needed.

Kenny went into the phone box while Brit stayed outside looking around, just taking in and observing the area, shops walkways, tracks, pubs, and anything else he thought we may need to be aware of. Kenny picked up the receiver, dialled the number Tony had written down for him, got his 10ps at the ready, and as the phone was picked up at the other end, Kenny started to feed the coins into it. He asked to be put through to BSM Bob of 58 battery.

"Who is calling please?" the duty clerk asked. "Gunner Dinsdale." The clerk didn't ask anything else, the phone seemed to go dead, then came the voice we all knew.

"Yes, what do you want? And it had better be good as I am heading home." It was BSM Bob. It wouldn't matter who was on the other end, he didn't care if he was heading home, he rarely let anything stop him – but this would. Although he had said he was dropping out of the team he would still do anything for us.

"It is Gunner Dinsdale, sir, I have been asked to contact you by Bdr Watt."

"Are you in location as instructed?"

"Yes, sir."

"OK Dinsdale, I'll not keep you on the phone, Donny and the rest of the lads will be with you tomorrow about 16:00 hours, so there will be 12 of you's on the task. They have all the information you will need, all you have to do until then is keep your heads down and try and suss out the area." As BSM Bob was telling him this, Kenny was trying to work out who the other seven were, as we only had ten in the team.

"Yes, sir, I have that."

"Good lad." Then the phone went dead.

Kenny pushed the heavy door open and looked at Brit.

"What is it?" Brit asked.

"I've just spoken to Bob and he said there was another seven joining us tomorrow."

"*Seven?*" Brit said. "Who are they?"

"He didn't say. Who do you think they could be? Do you think BSM Bob and Ian Tate will be the two extra? That's if Ian has convinced Bob to join us again."

On the way back to the house they stopped at a corner shop to pick up something for tea. As they headed back Brit was pointing out things he had observed. At the harbour was about four fishing boats, a fish market and a truck yard. He suggested they could get jobs there as a cover, and as it's heavy work it could be a place doormen might work. Kenny knew he was right, as he came from Hartlepool and that is a fishing town and a lot of the doormen worked in the industry. By the time they got back to the house, Glenn, me and Tony had checked out the three houses; we knew we would need a control room, and all agreed the big bedroom in the middle house was the best place. We would have two on stag at a time and four in each of the end houses. It wasn't until Kenny informed us that there were twelve of us altogether, that we realised it would be better as that meant more to share the stags. We all thought the same, the two others would be Bob and Ian. Brit put the shopping onto the bench and headed upstairs to the toilet. Little did I know that this was his way of saying he wasn't going to do the cooking. I got the look off the rest of them: it was *me* that was to do tea. I didn't mind, I quite enjoyed cooking.

When I emptied the bags, there was a bag of potatoes, fish fingers, and tins of beans, bread and butter, not very adventurous, but they didn't think to get lard to make chips, so mash it was. As we sat having tea Glenn got up and headed to the car. He grabbed a case of lager he'd picked up at the service station earlier that day. That was all we needed, food and drink and we were all happy. There was nothing else we could do, so we all sorted out our kit, and settled down for the night with the TV and drinks – that was until I asked if Kenny and Brit had found a fish and chip shop. I was hungry again, but that wasn't unusual, I loved my food, and fish and chips for supper is the best. Unfortunately they hadn't seen one. It was now dark and I thought it would be

OK for us to go out and we wouldn't be recognised if Big Bob was in the area. So me and Tony headed out.

We decided to head down to the harbour area, hopefully we would find a fish and chip shop down there, but nothing. As we started heading back up the hill towards the house I got a smell of a fish shop. As they say, follow your nose and you will find food, and we did. We had passed it on the way in as we followed Bill on his bike, but we were all too busy laughing about three cars following a pedal bike.

Back at the house with five fish and chips and a bag of batter; you can't beat a bag of batter with your chips, although some of the lads hadn't heard of it before, it was a northern thing. And we didn't forget the red sauce. We still had bread left from tea, so we were set for the night. Before we had finished supper we had finished the case of beer.

At about 23:00 hours we headed off to bed for the night, and got ready for the next day. We decided to all stay in the middle house for the night and sort out who would go where when the rest of the lads turned up.

The next morning I was up about 05:00 hours thinking of who the other two lads would be. Would it be BSM Bob and Ian, or two new lads? I couldn't think who else it could be. I looked out of the window in the living room, it was a bit overcast and the wind was blowing. Not surprising really as it was now the middle of October and the weather was starting to cut in. As I put my coat on, Kenny came down the stairs. "E up Geordie, you off home mate?"

"Just going for a walk mate."

"Give me five minutes and I'll join you."

"Yes mate, I'll sit on the wall and wait for you."

Kenny put his shoes on and grabbed his coat. As I sat on the wall, I started to think about Mam and Dad; what had Freddy said to Dad and what had Dad said to Mam. If there was one thing I didn't like, it was Mam getting upset, she worked so hard to look after the family, and the last thing I wanted was Mam having me on her mind. Kenny banged the door shut behind him, so if the rest of the lads hadn't already been awake, they would be now.

We set off down the cut towards the harbour area, we didn't think Big Bob would be out at this time in the morning, so we didn't have the fear of being seen. I could feel the cold air blowing around my neck, so I pulled up my hood and zipped up my coat.

Kenny asked if I was OK from the beating I took in the moors.

"Yes mate, doing OK, you?"

"Yes mate, just it keeps coming back that I felt so helpless when you took the kicking just before we got set loose."

"Don't let it get to you mate, that's in the past, we have to look forward, and remember if we get to catch Big Bob we both can get our own back."

We had walked more than we had both realised; before we knew it we were on the harbour and among the fishermen. Two fishing boats had just landed, there was a wagon parked up alongside the boats, there were two men on each boat, two on the harbour and two on the wagons. They were working well together: two boxes of fish would be dropped on the harbour, the two lads would pick up one at a time onto the wagon, and the lads on the wagon would slide them to the back of the wagon, and when they had enough they would go and stack them – and then they would all repeat the process. Just as I thought it was going so well for them, the two lads on the harbour bent down to pick up a box, and over came the hoist from the boat and caught one of them on the back of the head. Down he went. I felt the blow myself. Kenny ran across, he could see what was going to happen, but was too late to stop it. He grabbed the box and stopped it from swinging around, and I grabbed the lad, his head was split open, and the gash was quite deep; the lad was out cold. I grabbed him under the arms and dragged him clear so it didn't come down on him; his mate just stood looking. I think he was taken by surprise, as me and Kenny must have come from nowhere to him.

After I'd got the lad clear I checked his head, it was a bad cut, it was a hospital job as it may be infected from the fish covered box. The two lads on the wagon jumped to help. I got one of them to run and call an ambulance, off he went. He ran straight to the office that was on the side of the fish sheds. Just after he ran in, out came a well set man, about 6ft 2 and about 17 stone. It turned out he was the boss and the lad's dad. He had a first aid kit in his hand. "Do you need this?" he called out as he made his way over.

I knelt up and looked over to where the voice came from. "Yes please mate," I called out.

The man handed it to me. "Are you a doctor?" he asked.

It is strange what people say when they are in a panic.

"No mate, just first aid trained." I grabbed the kit out of his hand as he approached me, took out a bandage and some sterile wipes. He turned and saw Kenny unhooking the boxes onto the harbour. The lad that had been working on the harbour was in shock, one of the other lads took him into the office for a cuppa. Kenny got the other lad off the wagon to help him put the fish boxes onto the back of the wagon. When the ambulance arrived I informed the paramedic what had happened and what I had done to assist the lad. We then helped to put him into the ambulance. Just as we got him in, he started to come around. His dad was relieved. One of the paramedics checked out the other lad before leading him to the ambulance, after which they drove off to the hospital.

Kenny asked the rest of the lads, as they were now two men down, if they needed a hand.

"No lads, you've done enough for us by helping the young lad."

"How you going to work with just the four of you's?"

"We'll just have to do our best."

"No lads, we don't mind helping, let's get on with it," I insisted.

As me and Kenny walked toward the boat, we both thought the same: free fish for tea tonight. As the lads got back into the work position, me and Kenny stood on the harbour watching for the first boxes coming off the boat, grabbed them, unhooked them, and grabbed the two together and lifted them onto the wagon. The look on the lads' faces was a picture. *Lifting* the two boxes was not the done thing, as they are quite heavy, but to us it wasn't anything special, the workouts we did was just this type of thing. We would lift big rocks, uneven objects and heavy weights. After we had finished the lads thanked us, and as we started to walk away I said, "I hope your mate is doing OK."

"*Hang on lads*," one called out, "I'll give you a bit fish for your tea" (just as we hoped).

"You don't have to lads," Kenny said. I thought if they

don't give us any I'll nack him, but he had that smile on his face as if to say, *don't panic Geordie I know they wouldn't let us leave without fish.* One of them got a plastic bag out of the wagon and filled it with fish. As he was filling it, his mate asked if we liked crabs. YES, I said straight away. Crabs was one of my favourite sea foods.

I remember Dad bringing them to the caravan whenever we stayed there. He would boil them and get me and my brother Micky to shell them. Mam would always have a nipper, we could have the legs – not a lot of meat on them, but that didn't bother us, it was a bit extra food. Nine kids, so you would be grateful for anything you got on top of your dinner.

The lads had put enough fish in the bag to feed the 5000, they shook our hands, we thanked them and headed off. The time was now getting on, 7:30 hours and there were now people walking about heading to work. The lads would be wondering where we had got to.

"I think we just made some good friends there Geordie."

"I think you're right mate, let's hope we don't have to call on them for help, but if we do I think it could be useful."

As we got back to the house, the rest of the lads had all washed and had been starting to wonder where we had got to. As I was telling them what had happened Tony went off it. "Are you *stupid?*" he cried. Kenny couldn't understand why he reacted in such a way.

"You might have been seen, and what would we do then?"

I had thought of it but didn't think it was a problem, but to be fair, if we had been seen by Big Bob, that would be it. So I apologised and understood where Tony was coming from. Out of all of us, me, Kenny, Tony and Brit would be the ones that Bob would remember. Donny as well, but he wasn't with us at the moment. Brit asked what we had in the bags. Fish and crabs boys, was the answer.

"And what the fuck do you do with the crabs?" Brit asked.

"*Cook* them! What do you think?"

"Well, you'll have to do that Geordie," he said. "As I haven't got a clue with crabs."

We took them into the kitchen and I got out a big pan, dropped three crabs into it, and put them on the gas. Kenny got out the fish and me and him started to gut them. Glenn was in the living room looking at a map of the area, Tony and Brit joined him, and left me and Kenny with the fish. Gutting them was easy, we'd been shown how to gut fish on survival training, but also, me and Kenny had grown up with fish and fishing. Kenny would head to the docks in Hartlepool where he grew up (that was normal instead of going to school), he would nick a few off the wagons as they would be getting loaded. Me, I would be at Amble on the Northumberland cost, mostly with Dad and brother Micky, fishing, or Dad would get some off the boats as they came into the harbour.

By the time we had finished gutting the fish, the crabs were ready, so I put them on the drainer until we would eat them later. We then headed back into the living room. By this time Glenn, Tony and Brit were all looking over the map. Tony thought Glenn should go out and call camp, just to see if the rest of the lads had set off, and to see if Bob was on the other end of the phone. If he was, then the two extra lads wouldn't be Bob and Ian.

Glenn grabbed his top coat, pulled on his hat and set off, Tony chucked the keys of the other two houses to me and got Brit to go with me to check them out properly.

We headed for the end house first. As we opened the front door, we saw the stairs were straight ahead, a door to the living room was to the right, through the living room was a dining room, off to the left of that was the kitchen, a small galley-type one, with a back door leading to a large back garden. The fence at the end of the garden was about six foot tall. Brit walked down to it and looked through a hole in one of the planks. On the other side was an open field with a large wood at the far end. There were houses running down both sides of the wood, and they all looked like large mansion-type homes. We headed back inside and upstairs. There was one bathroom with a separate toilet, three good sized bedrooms, each had two single beds in and in the other was a double. So there was room for five (or six if someone was prepared to share – but that wasn't going to be me. One or two nights I could handle, but weeks or months *not a chance*). We headed back downstairs and over to the last house, which was very similar to the end one but on a smaller scale. One thing I had noticed was all back and front gardens had joining gates, so if we did do any moving around at night we wouldn't have to go up and down the street.

By the time me and Brit got back to the middle house, Glenn had returned. We all waited to see what he had to say. "The rest of the lads should be here between 13 and 14:00 hours, BSM Bob has took the address, and Dunc is to contact camp when he is about one hour outside of the town."

So, the two new lads were not Bob and Ian, but none of us could think who they could be. All had a chat about what

Tony had said about me, Brit and Kenny keeping out of sight. What was the point of us being there if we couldn't help? There was only one man that would have a clue how we were, so the decision was made. We would be out there with the rest of the lads, better be extremely careful not to draw attention to ourselves.

I decided to de-shell the crabs, and Kenny and Tony decided to head back down to the harbour so Tony could have a look about, and to see if there was a different way back up to the house, just in case it was needed.

As they were walking down the road towards the harbour, a car pulled up alongside them. The two of them got a bit of a shock, and stepped back as if to be ready to fight. It was the father of the young lad that had been taken to hospital early in the day. He wound down the window, stuck his hand out towards Kenny and said,

"Thank you for your quick reaction today boy, if it hadn't been for you and your friend, my son could have been in a lot more danger."

"That's OK," Kenny said, "but it was my other mate that helped your son, so it's him that should be thanked."

"Well, please pass on my thanks, and if there's anything I can do for you's, let me know."

At that point Tony piped up, "Yes, there is mate, you could give them a job on the docks."

Kenny looked at Tony as if to say, *shut it, let's not push our luck.*

"Well, that shouldn't be a problem, my son is going to be off work for a while, so I need one to cover him, and as for your mate, I only have a job for a couple of weeks but it is driving a forklift."

"Geordie can do that," Tony said confidently.

"Do you think so?" the man asked, not so sure.

"Yes, he drove a forklift at the steelworks he worked at before ..." he paused, as he was about to say 'the army', however, he changed it quickly to 'joining us'. The man then introduced himself.

"I'm Alan, so pop down tomorrow and I'll see what we can do boys." As he pulled away he waved his arm out the window.

Tony looked at Kenny, "This could be good for us, so don't blow it." They couldn't wait to get back to tell us, but decided to finish their walk first. As they walked they didn't speak a lot as they both were thinking of this great chance. Getting to know local people is always good when there are things going on; you can pick up a lot from local gossip.

Tony and Kenny hadn't returned before the rest of the lads arrived. A van and two cars pulled up outside the house. I heard a van door slam shut and looked out of the window. Glenn had stood up to check as well. I called out *"THE BOYS ARE HERE LADS."* Brit had been in the kitchen making a cuppa for us.

Dunc was the first out of the van, Jock and Donny got out of the front car and Platty out of the driver's side of the van – that meant the back car that we couldn't see from the window would have Evo and the two new boys in. But *who?*

Brit headed for the front door, with Glenn and me following close behind. Dunc was at the gate, as we stepped outside. I looked towards the last car. I couldn't believe my eyes. The two lads I last expected to join us, both from 58 Battery, probably the two lads you would ask for if you had to choose, Scouse Fargin and Smeet. We learnt later that their full names were Patrick Fargin and Mark Smeeton. It was strange but we never knew anyone's first names to begin with. The first time I ever heard any of their first names, was when Brit, Kenny and me had been locked in the hut out in the Yorkshire moors.

I remember Brit and Kenny chatting, Kenny asking Brit what his first name was. Mark he'd said. I sat thinking, I am probably going to die in the next day or two with the two of them, and I didn't even know their full names. I made a point of getting to know all the lads' names from then on. Scouse was one of the lads I was apprehensive about the most in the regiment, he was one of the lads you couldn't read. The first time I had really spoken to him, was in the garage back in Kirton Lindsey. He'd been telling me about his love for scratching. I didn't have a clue what he was on about, so he invited me to call to his room after work and he would show me. That was when I found out he wasn't one you could read, but we seemed to get on anyhow, and that was enough for me. The more lads I got on with, meant the less that would potentially bully me.

I remember my first day in the regiment, I got the train to Scunthorpe and jumped a taxi to the camp, got out at the gate, and on guard duty at the gate was a big set lad, I now know to be Charlie Spate. I walked up to him, and said I had to report to the duty sergeant. Are you Geordie Gordon, he asked me. Yes staff, I said. (In training you had to call everyone *staff*.) The words out of his mouth set my heart racing, sweat started to run down my back, and the fear I had at school came rushing back – this was going to be hell. I was wishing I had never joined the army, I could feel myself going weak at the knees. *SCOUSE FARGIN IS GOING TO FUCK YOU!* Who the hell was Scouse Fargin? I had never heard of him, or even seen him before. As he walked me to the guard room I was shaking.

He pushed the door open, and called out Gunner Gordon is here Sergeant, then he held the door open with his hand and stepped to one side for me to go in ahead. As I did the door closed behind me, Charlie hadn't come in behind me, but had headed back to his post on the gate. So *you* are Geordie Gordon the sergeant said. Shit, it seemed *everyone* knew who I was, but why and how? When I replied with *yes staff,* he shouted out *RUNNER,* and a short stocky lad appeared from a door at the side of the guard room.

"Yes Sergeant," the lad called out.

"Fargin, take this lad to 58 battery office to see BSM Wilson."

SHIT! This was Fargin.

"Yes Sergeant," he replied and headed towards me. As we left the guard room, Charlie was stood by the gate with a big grin on his face. Scouse looked at him, "You been winding them up again?" It turned out that Charlie was the regiment's wind up merchant. Scouse looked at me. "He had you there, didn't he?" "Yes staff," I replied. "You're not in training now mate, stop with the staff, I'm a gunner the same as you, and the rest you call by their ranks." He took me to the battery offices and seemed to calm me down on the way. He introduced me to the BSM, and headed back to the guard room to complete his duty. As he left he called out, "I'll see you in the block later mate." That sounded good, I may have made a friend on the first day, and that felt good.

As it happened we became good friends. Smeet was

my first number one I had been attached to; 21D the sub unit, that was my first Rapier unit and the one I had in the Falklands. Smeet taught me a lot about the regiment and the equipment I was now assigned to – he even got me onto the regiment football team.

That was all when I was a 'nig' in the regiment, but now that was in the past, and we all had a different role now, working together in this sort of job was a lot different, and that's what we did. I got on well with Scouse and Smeet, and I learnt a lot from them, not just great lads but top soldiers.

We all started to help them with the kit out of the cars and van. I headed to the van first, Evo followed me. "Don't open the back doors Geordie," he called out. I turned and looked at him with a puzzled look on my face. As he approached me, he said in a soft spoken voice, "The van has a side door, use that mate and you'll see why." As he slid the door open, I understood why. The kit bags had been stood by the door. As I grabbed one, I looked in the back of the van, it was like something off the TV – the Sweeney came to mind – the van was kitted out with all sorts of equipment for observation recording and tracking. We all had to be trained on it, and Scouse was the one to do it, he had been on so many courses that if anyone needed an answer to anything he would have it. Lying on the floor were about four or five different signs for the sides of the van, that were to be changed for the different locations the van would be parked.

Just as we had finished unpacking the van, all radio equipment went straight upstairs and into the back bedroom. We had to set up a coms room, as this was going to a big operation, a lot bigger than we all had thought. Just as we sat down to a cup of tea, the front door opened, and in came Kenny and Tony. Kenny was over the moon.

Scouse and Smeet had taken Kenny under their wing the first day he arrived at the regiment. Kenny was a cheeky lad, but funny with it, and it was the sort of humour they both liked. Kenny jumped straight onto Scouse with his daft sort of messing around; they hugged and appeared over the moon to see each other. Once we settled down, Smeet piped up to remind us we were on a job out here, and so we all needed to remember it was not an exercise. Just then I realised that Chris was missing.

"Did Chris not come with you lot?"

"He was asleep in the back of one of the cars," Evo piped up. At that all the lads had a good old laugh, we all knew what Chris was like at sleeping, he would drop off anywhere he could. Tony wasn't impressed. "This is *not* a game lads, Geordie, go and fetch him."

As I approached the car, Chris's head slowly rose above the back window. I could see the funny side of it, but Tony was right, this wasn't a game, this could be life or death if we got it wrong, we all had to switch on from now on, and all games or messing around had to stop – at least until we all got into the job, and knew what we would have to do.

I had decided to take charge of the coms room. I got Scouse and Brit to give me a hand, up the stairs we went. As we got into the room, Scouse headed straight for the window and pulled the curtains shut. We then had a good look over the equipment, a lot of it was stuff we hadn't seen before, but the instructions where self-explanatory. We cracked on with it and had it up and running in about 2½ hours. We had coms with camp and Hereford, and all we had to do now was get coms with the van and two of the five cars. Evo and Smeet were working on the van, and Dunc and the rest of the lads had started on the rest of the equipment that was in the living room. Getting everything ready was essential, we couldn't make any mistakes. This was a big job and our lives would be jeopardised if any one of us got it wrong, so going over and over the equipment was just one of the things we had to do.

Having finished in the coms room, Smeet decided to go and have a check to see if all was well. It was one of the things he always did, let you get on with it, but go over things just to be on the safe side (just as well at times, because things *did* go wrong every now and again) but this time we had got it right.

Downstairs in what had been a dining room, but was now a briefing room, Donny had a map laid on the table. It covered the area of Pembrokeshire, and it had all the pubs, clubs and restaurants marked out. This wasn't the type of map we would normally use, as this one had all areas named, streets and even hospitals, though the one thing Dunc noticed was that there was no police station, and the military camp he knew was in the area, had also been left off the map. This was down to the IRA operating outside of Ireland; all military and government buildings had been left off all maps since the early 1970s.

After Smeet had checked the coms room, and was happy with it, he got us all into the meeting room, and got Donny to go over the area he wanted to concentrate on first. Haverfordwest town centre was the first area and in particular the night life area, would probably be where Big Bob would be, or have contacts with. Platty went over the areas he had picked out as good cover areas, so if things got a bit out of hand, we could head for these, just to get out of the thick of things. There were now 13 of us and we would have to work in teams, one of six and one of seven. We would also break them down to twos and threes if needed. I said I thought some of us would have to try and get jobs, just as part of the cover, and Tony piped up with a further thought: "What about the docks? We spoke to the father of the lad Geordie gave first aid to this morning on the docks, he has a job Geordie and Kenny can do, it is out of the way and the only people they will see is fishermen, and I can't see Big Bob going down there if he is in the area."

Donny and Jock agreed, and Evo thought *free food, fish*. I wasn't too happy about it, but it went to a vote, and that was that. We had to go down the next day and have a chat with Alan, we all thought he had to be the boss, or at least a supervisor.

That night it had been agreed we would all head down into the town. We had been split up into twos and threes, and I had been paired with Scouse and Donny. We weren't really looking for anything in particular, apart from checking out the area where we thought things might happen. Evo and Jock were the first two to get dropped off; they were dropped on the main road, it was about one mile outside of the town. We knew they wouldn't be recognised, as Evo had just joined the team and Jock hadn't had contact with Big Bob. Chris had Smeet, and took one car with Glenn and Kenny. They dropped Glenn and Kenny outside a pub, hoping they wouldn't bump into Big Bob, but to be fair, even if he was in the area, we didn't think he would recognise us as we had let our hair grow, some had grown stubble and or a moustache. Once we were all in the area we had to look over, we just blended in – we were just some lads heading out for the night.

It was a Wednesday, so we had dressed down a bit. As we walked along one of the streets, I could feel the night air on my face, and hear the birds rustling in the trees trying to settle in for the night on the safest branch, the sun was just going down behind the trees, and there was a slight chill in the air. We soon came to a set of large gates on the left, and a row of big houses on the right. The houses looked expensive – the sort an officer would have – and on the gates was the name Haverfordwest Country Park. We decided to take a look in, nothing special, pretty much like the one back home, Saltwell Park in Gateshead.

We sometimes went to Saltwell Park with Uncle Richard and his mates, to fish in the lake. I say *fish*, but it was only with a net on the end of a thin cane, and a jam jar, but they were good times. Uncle Richard lived with us, nine kids, Mam and Dad, and three dogs, all in a three-bed semi-detached council house; seven girls in one room, Mam and Dad in the master room, Micky and me at the top of a single bed, and Uncle Richard in the bottom – it was cramped, but we survived.

We walked around for a while, and then I decided to head for the boundary fence, there was thick undergrowth for about ten yards from the path to the fence, large trees in among it. We slowly walked along the path until Donny stopped suddenly. "Look over there lads."

Scouse saw it straight away, but I couldn't. Wasn't sure where I was supposed to be looking.

"Out into the street," Scouse said, then the penny dropped. It was the club we would be doing the surveillance on. I could now see what he was thinking, *have an observation point in the thicket.* Donny now was looking into the thicket.

"Scouse, could you get in there, without disturbing the ground?"

"Not a problem, mate," he said, and at that he walked along the path, checking for fox runs. It didn't take him long to find one ... and in he went. It wasn't long before he disappeared out of sight. We kept look out for people coming along the path. Scouse was only in it for about fifteen minutes, before he popped out about 25 yards along the path. We walked towards him. "Well?" I said.

"Three good points in there, well covered and only about two feet off the road. There's no path on the park side of the road, so you wouldn't get people walking along."

"Yes, that's all well and good, but how will we get in, the park will have a time to lock up?" Donny said. "Let's head back to the gate and see if there's a lock up time on it."

We had a slow walk down to the entrance, and as luck would have it, there was a man with the keys checking his watch. "OK boys, you're lucky, I'm just about to lock up, you nearly had to walk to the bottom gate."

"Sorry, sir," I said, "we're just working in the area for a few weeks, and popped out for a look around."

"Well, we lock up at 7 o'clock every night from next week."

I looked at my watch, it was 19:55hours.

"But it's nearly 8," I said.

"Yes, that's right, boy." I was getting fed up with being called *boy* all the time, but that's what the Welsh did – every male got *boy* when spoken to. "From Saturday the time changes," he said. At that we thanked him and headed out of the park.

As we walked along the road, Scouse said, "We'll have to get someone in before it locks up."

"Yes mate," I said. "Getting out under dark is no problem, but going *in*. We can't take the chance climbing the fence in daylight, so we'll have to be in the park before lock-up. We'll have to decide who it'll be."

"I think it should be you Scouse," Donny said.

"No chance, I want to be in the action."

"Well, it'll be decided by the team, so I wouldn't worry at the moment mate," I said. "We'll all be given jobs off BSM Bob Wilson when the time is right."

We all had a good feeling about this area, it was more of a village than a town, so we all felt a little bit happier. Brit, Tony and Dunc walked the streets around the club, and found an ideal places to park the ops van. I hadn't really checked the van out, but one thing I had noticed, was there were two windows in the sides of it, a small one to the rear on the nearside, and a larger one on the offside, that one was more to the centre of the van. Both had one-way glass, to see out and not in, but I couldn't see how the signs could go on as they would cover the windows up. That was until I saw them proper. By this time we'd been out looking around for about three hours and so headed back to the pickup points before heading back to the houses.

As we pulled up in the street, we saw an old man checking his garden, so we headed into different houses, out the back doors and into the middle house. Me and Brit headed to the kitchen to make a cuppa for the team, and Smeet and Platty got the maps out and laid them on the table in the briefing room. Jock and Donny got out the notepads, to take notes on what we'd all picked up:

Dunc had seen a pub in the area he was looking over, it wasn't too far from the club, so he thought that would be the place the doormen would probably have a pint before starting work. Smeet went into his jacket pocket and pulled out five photos, all of Big Bob. As soon as I saw them, the hairs on my arms stood up, I got a shiver down my spine. I looked at Kenny and Brit, and could see they felt the same. Tony looked at me, and could see I wasn't happy about seeing Big Bob again. He didn't say anything but he knew I was full of anger. Donny told them about the find we had in the park, and after we had all put in our ten penneth, we sat back and milled over it all; we all had questions about different things, but me, Smeet and Jock put it all down on paper, headed to the ops room, and contacted camp.

Piper was on stag again, Ian had got him to cover it for the next two weeks, on the night shift. This would only be until the surveillance started, then BSM Bob and IAN would cover it. They didn't want anything to go wrong. BSM Welsh had been given the job of looking after the backup team, so he kept away from the coms room in camp.

We all left Jock and Smeet with the job of contacting camp, so I headed off to bed, ready for the next day on the docks – that was if we got the job, but by all accounts it was in the bag for us.

As I was walking back to one of the end houses I had a look into the street, and noticed the old man was still in his garden. It was just after midnight, and I thought he obviously had problems, probably early dementia, but I just left him to it and headed indoors.

I lay on top of the bed, just looking at the shadow from the street light, and thinking to myself about the task in hand. I couldn't get Big Bob out of my head; the thought of what he'd done to me, Brit and Kenny really grated on me, but the thing that got to me more was that he had double-crossed his own men, and had run off with the cash, left his men to fight what was probably something he'd got them into, *his* fight. I was desperate to have my time with him, but I knew Brit and Kenny felt the same. So when, or *if,*we got the chance, I hoped I would be the first in line ...

After a while I could hear someone coming up the stairs. I climbed into bed and turned over, as if to be asleep – I wasn't in the mood to chat.

The next day I was up at 06:00 hours and feeling a lot better, ready to start work on the docks, hopefully, that was if Alan would give us the job he had half promised. As I was getting dressed Tony woke. "Pop the kettle on, Geordie, that's a good lad."

"Up yours, get up and do it yourself you lazy git." He knew I would as we always did for each other. I headed downstairs and into the kitchen. Scouse and Evo were already in making breakfast.

"The kettle's just boiled, mate," Evo said, "and breakfast won't be long mate."

That was great, it saved me a job. I poured the tea for the four of us, and took them into the living room, drew back the curtains and sat on the armchair by the window. It looked fresh outside, the trees gently blowing in the morning breeze, the birds hopping around the garden, and the old man from along the street was out walking his dog. By the time Tony came downstairs Evo and Scouse had breakfast on the table, a full English, just what I needed. The four of us chatted as we ate, mostly about what we had seen the night before, just in case we had missed anything that might have been of any importance. Nothing came up. After we finished breakfast me and Tony cleaned up, we thought it only fair. It was now 07:25hours so we grabbed our coats and headed to the coms house, the middle one of the tree.

The rest of the lads were already sitting around the table, looking over the map again just to reassure themselves. At 08:00 hours it was time for me and Kenny to head down to the docks and look to see if Alan was around this early. We set off at the same time Brit and Chris decided to have a walk down into the village, just for a look around.

Me and Kenny walked through the cut, as Brit headed to the end of the street. When we hit the north side of the harbour, Kenny asked if I was OK. "Yes mate, why do you ask?"

"Last night when Big Bob was mentioned I noticed the look on your face had changed."

"I just can't stand the thought that that prick is out there, and he double-crossed his own men … and that he would probably be looking to get some poor young lad to do the same as he did to us."

"That's if we don't get to him first," Kenny replied.

We went over the bridge to the south side of the harbour. I looked over to the area where we had seen the lads working the day before, and I could see Alan walking towards a boat that was trying to dock.

"It looks like the first job of the day has just arrived mate," I said.

Alan was helping two lads to tie the boat up to the harbour, and load a wagon that was reversing towards the harbour side. As we approached Alan called out, "Am I glad to see you boys, you come for a job?"

"Yes mate," I said, "if you have any." We knew he had, but it sounded better than being cocky, and saying yes, where do you want us to start. "Good," he called out, "can you lift the boxes from the harbour to the wagon for the lads and after you have done that, come over to the office and we can have a chat." Well, that told me straight away, he had no intention of working with us to load the wagon, but that didn't matter as long as we got work and had the chance to keep out of trouble. And back at the house things would look more normal to the neighbours.

As soon as the lads had the boat secured to the harbour, we got on with it, it only took about half an hour to complete the job, and the lads thanked us. Good to have someone who works, which I took as if to say, Alan's son didn't do much, or didn't work hard. "Well, thanks lads," I said.

"Will there be any more boats in today?" Kenny asked.

"Yes, we should have about nine all together, all before dinner, then after dinner we start on the sorting, weighing and pricing." We didn't expect that. We thought we would be just loading and unloading the boats, but no. "Alan will want to get his money's worth out of you. You'd better go and see Alan as he asked, he can be a bit of a twat if you don't do as he asks."

Kenny looked at me, and we both headed off towards the office. As we walked I lit up a tab, and Kenny said, "Let him start with me and he'll be sorry." I just laughed at him. Kenny would always come out with a fight comment, and never follow it up, but to be fair, when someone did get his back up, they would know about it.

I recall one time when we were in training together. Two of the lads that had decided the army wasn't for them still had to stay until the paperwork had been sorted. Each night when we all would be doing the block jobs, in they would come and start having a go at some of the littler lads. One night Kenny had finished his jobs and had climbed into bed. I was up the other end of the block in a different room, when one of the lads from Kenny's came running up to me (I was the troop leader for the week). "You'd better come Geordie," he called out. "The dicks are having a go at Kenny!" *Dicks* is what we had named the two nomads. I ran straight down to the room, but it was too late, the two of them were lying on the floor at the side of Kenny's bed, and Kenny was in his bed. The rest of the lads were stood at the bottom of the room. Blood was all over the floor.

"*WHAT THE HELL HAS HAPPENED HERE LADS?*" I looked at Kenny.

"Well, they shouldn't pick on me."

It turned out, Kenny had fallen asleep, and the two nomads had tried to squirt shaving foam into his mouth. Kenny had leapt out of bed, smashed one of the lads with his bedside locker, and the other with his iron across the face. I can say we had no more trouble from them.

As we got to the office I flung me tab and opened the door, Kenny lead the way. Alan was sat behind a large desk with a phone and a radio sat at either side of it, and a large book in front of him; he was puffing on a big cigar as he called out

"Come in boys and take a seat". I closed the door behind me and walked to the chair in front of the desk, Kenny grabbed one from the corner of the room and pulled it next to me. "Well, that didn't take you lads long."

I thought of saying yes, the lads said we work hard, not like your son, but thought better of it. I'd noticed a forklift on the way from the dock to the office, at the side of the sheds, so instead I said,

"Do you not use the forklift that is out there?"

"We would if the dicks hadn't broken it." I took it 'the dicks' were the lads that worked for him. Me and Kenny both felt that he had no respect for the lads that worked for him, however we didn't know them to judge. They might be dicks, but we would find out soon enough.

"What's wrong with it? I may be able to fix it for you."

"The hydraulics have gone, so unless you have a strong pipe I don't think so, although I do have an old forklift in the back of the shed. You could see if there's anything on that that might help you."

"No problem, mate," I said.

"I'm *NOT* your mate," he said in a sturdy voice, "I'm your *BOSS*," then he laughed. "Just joking boy, you call me Alan."

If you keep calling me boy, you'll end up with a bent nose! I thought to myself, best not say it aloud though, as we need the job.

"Give me a moment," he said as he picked up the radio. He called one of the fishing boats, checking the time it would arrive at the dock. He checked his watch and looked at me. "You have one hour before it comes in, so if you could have a look at the forklift I'd appreciate it."

"No problem," I said. "Do you have the keys?"

He pulled open the drawer on the left side of the desk and pulled out a bunch of keys. "It'll be on there somewhere boy," as he threw them at me.

I had to try and ignore this thing of *boy*. I could see Kenny smirking, he knew that it got to me. I grabbed the keys and headed for the door, Kenny followed. As we got outside Kenny broke down laughing.

"Your face mate," he said.

"*BOY, up yours!*" I said back to him, but I could see the funny side, and I started laughing with him.

The forklift was a Hyster. Great, I thought, I'd worked on them before, when I worked at the steelworks back in Gateshead. Before I looked through the keys, I had a good look at the two trucks. I didn't think it would be a problem, and we cracked on with it until the next boat arrived. The day seemed to go quickly and before we knew it, it was home time. I took the keys back to the office and informed Alan that I would have the forklift on the road by the end of the following day. "Good job you've done today lads, thank you." We must be getting somewhere, I thought, he didn't call me boy!

While we had been working some of the lads had been in contact with camp. BSM Ian had had a chat with BSM Bob and convinced him to join us on the *mission in the field* as we called it. That was great. He was from the area and it would be a great help to the whole operation.

Brit had been out most of the day on his own, just checking out the area around where we were living. There were only three pubs and one working man's club that he could find, so he thought if two or three of us headed down that evening, we could get a feel for the area, and its people. Smeet and

Tony had headed into the main town Haverfordwest, with Evo and Dunc, while Jock and Platty had gone to the shops to get more food as there were more mouths to feed. Donny was on cooking duties, so he stayed in. Scouse had decided to head back to the park he had checked out the night before.

As he checked the hide he had found the previous evening, he also saw a second one in a garden at the side of the club we were keeping a check on. It was an office block garden with overgrown bushes and a thick hedgerow. This was ideal for surveillance, probably better that the one in the park, so it was decided that we would use them both, as they thought it best for me to be out of the way for now. I was in one and Brit and Tony would be in the other one. If Big Bob was in the area he would recognise Tony for definite – Tony and BSM Bob were the two that had been visiting the club in Lincolnshire when me, Brit and Kenny had been kidnapped. Donny was also ruled out, as he had been working the doors with Big Bob to get inside information, but like the coward Big Bob was, he double-crossed his own men and ran off with the cash.

When we all got back to the house at the end of the day, tea was on the go – it smelt lovely. Donny wasn't a bad cook, but he didn't enjoy that job, he would always prefer to be in the action. After tea we all gathered in the briefing room, to go over the plan for the night. Smeet, Tony and Dunc had been selected to run the show for the first night, although Smeet and Tony had the rank, it didn't matter to any of us, as we always worked as a team, and took ideas from each other, and worked things out as a team. If it was ever needed, they would pull rank, but that was very rare. Donny had to remain indoors and man the radios; Scouse, Evo and Jock would head to the club; Glenn would take Kenny and Platty to one of the pubs in the village that Brit had suggested we do; Dunc and Chris would go to a different village pub, and then head to the working man's club; Tony and Donny would make contact with camp and get the full story on BSM Bob and his arrival. Smeet informed us that BSM Ian Tate would be running things from camp, and he had a backup team in hand if it was required.

Me and Brit headed off to get ready for a cold night ahead of us. As we were packing the bags, Brit said, "I thought Scouse was supposed to do this shit."

"Yes, that's what I thought as well mate, but to be fair, it does make sense us doing it. I think Big Bob may recognise us if he did see one of us."

"Not a chance mate," Brit retorted. "Did you not see the state of us after the kicking? And Big Bob hadn't seen us before that." Brit was right, but it is what it is, we just had to get on with it. The rest of the lads had headed off to get ready for a night on the piss, but I hadn't even bothered to get washed – you always try to have a natural smell about you when you're in a hide, and any smells of deodorant or soap could give the game away, especially in an area of houses and pubs.

The time had been getting on, it was now 20:00 hours and Scouse and Evo had got the keys for two of the cars. They had agreed to meet in the pub down the street from the club. Me and Brit got a lift off Evo while Jock and Scouse went on ahead.

When we arrived in town, we noticed there weren't many people about. We knew it would be quiet as it was a Thursday night, but it was all just a dummy run. We parked the car in one of the side streets by the park. Evo handed Brit the keys, as we would not be leaving until all the clubbers and staff had left. Evo then headed off and left us to it. We knew the park would be locked up for the night, as we had spoken to the parky the day before. We had to try and get in as close as possible to the hide area. We had an idea where Brit would get in, but we didn't want to look too suspicious walking around, so as we approached it, we slowed down, checked around and made a bolt for it.

First his backpacks went over the fence, then I gave Brit a leg up. Down he went, grabbed the bags and jumped into the hedgerow. As I was about to move off to my hide area, I spotted a man walking his dog, heading in my direction. I bent over and started to fasten my laces, the oldest trick in the book, but for some strange reason it works every time. Brit lay still as the man passed, and as I headed away from the area, I checked that the man wasn't looking, then ran back to check Brit was OK. I left him to it and headed off to my hide in the garden of the office building.

I checked it out from the outside of the fence, waited for it to be clear, and leaped off the metal fence, crawled under the hedge and waited for a while. I thought I should sit there for a while, just until it had got completely dark. So that's what I did. When it got to 20:45hours I decided to move.

Glenn and his team had got to the pub for about 20:10 hours and seemed to hit it off with the locals. As normal they had headed for the pool table, that seemed to be the best place to make friends. They stayed until 22:35hours and then thanked the lads for the game and making them welcome. They agreed to meet them the next night, as it seemed the way to get information and possible invites to hit the town with them. If you headed into clubs with the locals you seemed to blend in more, but if you headed into a club as a bunch of strangers, you got noticed by everyone.

Dunc and Chris didn't have the same sort of luck, the club was full of old men, all playing cards, dominoes and darts, so they headed to one of the other pubs, the Leek and Dragon. All the pubs had names like the Prince of Wales, the Queen's head, the Dragon's Head, the George and Dragon, typical Welsh names. Still, no luck at that one either. But Evo and his team had a bit more luck, the pub was full of lads and lasses just waiting for the club to get started.

As the first clubbers headed off to the club, Evo's team followed, they needed to be one of the first lot in as they needed to have good seats, to observe the whole area in the club. However, they didn't want to be in too soon that they would be noticed. As they entered the club, they were met by three doormen. "OK boys?" one of them asked, "you not from around here are you?"

Scouse piped up, "No, we're here looking for work."

"There's plenty down here boys, you shouldn't have any trouble finding it."

"Thanks mate," Scouse said, "could you give me any names or companies I could get in touch with mate?"

"Yes, you get yourself in and I'll catch up with you later."

That seemed good, if we could do the same as we'd done at Lincoln, get someone on the inside, that would be fantastic, but luck like that never happens twice.

In they went, and Jock spotted a booth over the far side of the club.

Ideal he thought, no one behind us, close to the bar, and all round vision. Jock and Scouse headed for the booth while

Evo had the first shout at the bar. As the club started to fill up, the operation they had was brilliant. The club was on three levels, the booths on the outer sides in a horse shoe, the next level was the same, but no booths just tables, and then there was a standing area around the dance floor. It wasn't that full, with it being a Thursday most would be waiting for the weekend, but it gave us a great opportunity to observe the club, and the areas the doormen covered. The doormen started to have a bit of a dig at some of the young lads, you could see they thought it was clever and made them look impressive to the young girls. Scouse was always one that would have the girls after him (I hate to say it, but he was a bit of a looker).

Jock got up to go to the bar just as a fight broke out. He stepped back and looked back at Scouse and Evo. Evo shook his head; he knew what was in Jock's mind, *fight lads, let's get stuck in,* that would be the norm, but they had a job to do and couldn't mess it up, so he just watched and checked out the bouncers. As the norm, there is always one or two that get stuck in, and the ones that hold back a bit, just to check out the opposition. That was good for us, as if it kicked off in the club with us, we had an idea who to hit first. They all seemed to head for one lad, but it wasn't him that started it. They dragged him outside, and at this point, Evo headed out to see what was going on, and what they would do with him. The poor kid didn't stand a chance, his girlfriend was sobbing, not a thing she could do.

But it was good for us. The lads had gained a lot, on the night, and had some phone numbers to ring in the morning for jobs. The more of us that had jobs, the better chance of information we could get. One of the doormen had come to their table with the list of phone numbers for them. One, he said, was his dad's company so it was a good chance to become pally with him. As he worked for his dad as well, Jock asked what the fight had been about, and said he couldn't believe the little lad was the one that started it. He knew he hadn't, but he was after a reaction.

"He didn't start it, but the other lads spend a lot of cash here, and the big one in the red top …" he said as he pointed over to where the man was standing, "… his dad is the local hard man, so we don't mess with him." Scouse thought he would have a pop at getting something out of him as well.

"So, I thought you doormen are the hard lads?"

"We can handle ourselves, but his dad says who does what in this area."

This was all good information and a big help to us.

"So is his dad the owner of the club?"

"No, it's part of a chain by some company up north, I think it is called The Good Brewers."

Jock had heard of it, but from where he couldn't remember – he didn't think it was important.

Me and Brit on the other hand, were stuck in a 'basher' freezing our nuts off. We stayed in the hide until 03:30 hours.

The club had all locked up and there was nothing for us to report, neither of us had seen anything to report, apart from the one fight with the doormen. It did look a bit of a shame for the young lad, but the kicking he got wasn't the same as Brit, Kenny and me had suffered. Me and Brit had arranged to meet back at the car if things didn't develop. As soon as we got in the car we headed home.

On the way we chatted, but it was more about the hides – how they could be improved and more importantly, how we could get out of doing another night in them. When we got back home, the place was in darkness. I headed straight to bed as I had to be up for work on the docks by 07:00 hours.

The next morning I was up by 06:30 hours. Tony wasn't in his bed so I took it he had gone down to make breakfast. After I got showered and dressed, I headed downstairs. As I'd thought, Tony was in the kitchen with the bacon on the go.

"Kettle has just boiled mate," he said, "anything last night?"

"No mate, it was just another night at a club from me and Brit, what about Evo and his lads?" I asked.

"Don't know mate, I was in bed by the time they got home, but we'll be having a meeting later this morning."

"Well, me and Kenny will miss it, we have work at 08:00 hours until 16:00 hours."

"Don't worry, we'll be having a second meeting tonight, before we head out for more observation on the club."

Just as I was leaving to knock on Kenny, Scouse and Evo came into the kitchen. "You off Geordie?" Scouse asked.

"Yes mate, off to work, not like you lazy bunch."

"I'll have you know mate, I may have a job myself today," Evo said. I stopped in the doorway as I was leaving, "*Yes?*"

"Well hopefully," he said. "We got a few numbers off one of the doormen so could have work by the end of the day."

"Good luck," I said, and left.

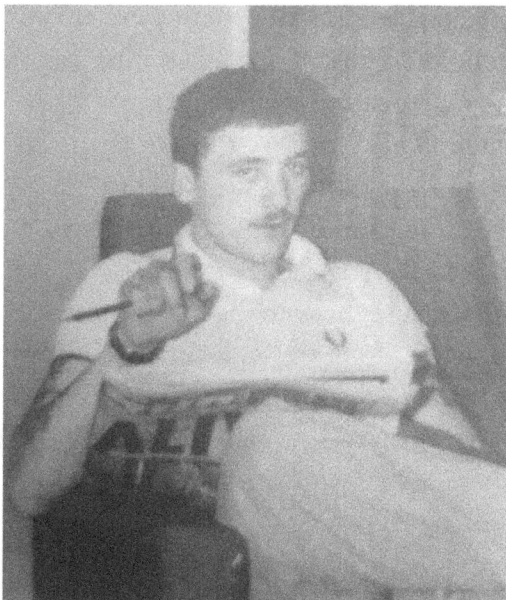

Kenneth Dinsdale (Ward)

(Kenny)

Royal Artillery, 1981 to 1985

When I approached Kenny's he was already at the door waiting for me. "Well," he said, "anything last night mate?"

"No mate, just a cold night and one daft fight at the club but nothing to write home about."

"Yes, us the same mate, apart from we got chatting with some lads and have arranged to meet them tonight for a drink. What about Evo's team?"

"Yes, they got some numbers to ring for work, well, at least they might get work, so it's not just us that will be bringing home the cash."

As if that really mattered, we all get paid from the army anyway.

When we arrived at work there were already two boats in waiting to be unloaded. We walked into the office and Alan and the lads were sitting having a cuppa.

"Morning lads," I said, as I took off my coat and hung it on the chair in the corner, "we ready to go?"

"Another ten minutes yet," one of them said.

"You're keen," Alan said.

"No mate, I just think if the job is there we should get on with it, and we can get on with the forklift quicker."

"Good idea, let's go lads." Kenny could see the lads looking at me as if to say, *you gobshite*. As we headed out one of the lads called me a gobshite. I turned and looked at him,

"You talking to me?"

"Yes, we don't get paid for starting early mate."

"No," I said "but if we crack on, we could start and ask if we could get away a bit sharper."

"Alan won't let us do that."

"Why not?" I asked.

"He's not the sort of bloke to give anything away."

"Don't you worry about him, I'll sort it with him."

We cracked on, got the fish all sorted, and I headed for the forklift. Before long I'd got it working and had taken some spares parts off the old one in the corner, cleaned them up and put them on a shelf in the shed. Kenny was working with the lads on the harbour. I left them to it and popped in to see Alan. "Well the forklift is working boss," I said.

"You're joking, you got it *going*?"

"Yes, and I have some spare parts on the shelf from the old one."

He jumped out of his seat. "Well, I'll have to see this."

I couldn't understand what the fuss was about, I had only fixed a forklift, not built him a boat. I handed him the keys, and he jumped on the truck and started it up, a big smile on his face, like a boy with a new toy. He drove around the harbour a few times and headed back into the shed, "Thank you, this has saved me a lot of cash."

Well, I thought this was the best time to cash in on it, "Well, how about letting us off work a little sooner today? The lads have also worked hard."

"Yes, why not."

It was only 14:20 hours, but he called the lads over.

"You've worked hard today lads, so off you go for the weekend, and enjoy yourselves."

The lad that had given me lip earlier in the day, looked over at me and winked, and mouthed *sorry*. It turned out he was called Paul and was a good lad, they had just let Alan take advantage of them and hadn't even tried to get any time back off him. Things changed from then on. We worked well together and had a good time with the lads, and I had given Alan more ideas on how to save cash, and get the best out of the lads.

Me and Kenny ended up working there for a while and made good money. Evo, Scouse and Smeet had got work from the lad in the club, but we didn't really get any information from them or any clues on what would be going on and where Big Bob was or had been. BSM Bob had decided not to come down until we had something to work on, or had information on Bob or some sort of action that was going to happen. We had started to use the van for stakeouts as well as the hides, and the lads all took turns on visiting the club – that also included me and the lads that had been on the last hunt. The van was brilliant and the equipment was fantastic. It had things I had never seen before, but we all got used to it, and I often observed from it. It was about three weeks in, we had all been taking turns on the stakeout of the club but nothing … that was until one night.

I was on the stakeout in the van. I had got a bed to relax over time and on that night I was thinking about the times I had been scared as a kid.

The kickings, the taunting, the humiliation, and the embarrassment it would have been for the family if they'd ever found out. The kickings didn't really scare me, it was more what would happen *after* the kicking that got to me. Also the taunting after was the bit I hated most. Everyone would join in and even if I could've beaten them in a fight, it wasn't worth it. One thing I do remember that frightened me the most was on a Sunday Dad would take two of us at a time to the baths. I did understand why, with nine kids it wouldn't be cheap to take us all at the same time. I would always go with my oldest sister Ann; Uncle Geordie Hall would also go with two of his kids. I say uncle, but Geordie was Dad's best mate, and we have always been like family (even now I think of them as family). The two Geordie took at the same time as me were Keith and Bobby, his only two boys. Geordie was the one that would teach us to swim, Dad wouldn't go in the water. I don't think he could swim. Geordie would get us to lay over his arms, kick our legs and breast stroke with our arms. I remember one time I had just about got the swimming, still scared of Uncle Geordie not being at my side, I was messing about in the shallow end of the pool with Keith and Bobby. I was OK as long as I could touch the bottom, but they'd somehow got me to go up to the deep end of the pool. I was standing on the side of the pool just watching them on the diving board. At the time I couldn't swim a lot, but Keith and Bobby had started jumping off the board, doing somersaults, twists and all kinds of things. I was impressed. I thought I would never be able to do that in a million years. Before I knew it, they'd both talked me into going on the board. As I walked to the end of the board it was hell. It wasn't the height, it was the water below. I remember seeing Keith in the water shouting at me to jump, and Bobby was at the side of the board. The next thing I remember was me under the water. Bobby had pushed me off the board, but the thing was he had also jumped in after me. I was shitting it.

I thought I was going to die. As my head bobbed above the water, I could see Keith and Bobby in the water at the side of me, calling out *SWIM JOHN, YOU CAN DO IT!* I was doggie paddling towards the side, and Bobby and Keith were there at the side of me all the way. I knew then they were there to help me, and it was that that got me swimming. I never did thank them, I was in shock at what had happened. I looked at Dad and he was clapping, so I knew I had done it. So thank you Keith and Bobby – what you did that day helped me later on in life (which I'll tell you about one day).

As I focused back on the job in hand, a car pulled up. It stopped outside the club doors. As the passenger got out I recognised him, but from where I couldn't remember … then the penny dropped. Smeet and Donny were in the van with me, and I remembered – it was David from the Good

Brewers in Scunthorpe. The lad with him I hadn't seen before but I had an idea it might be the lad that gave him the pub, but I couldn't remember his name. As he got out of the car he opened the back door and took out a parcel, it was in the shape of the picture frame. We didn't take much notice of it. Tony was in the club – that was dangerous. If he was spotted it could be trouble for him. He was wearing a wire so I contacted him to let him know. Tony and some of the lads were sitting in the seats we'd claimed the first time we'd entered the club. I started to get a bit anxious thinking this could be our cover blown if we weren't careful. All the lads had wires on, so they were all at the ready in case things kicked off.

I prayed things wouldn't, as that would be a massive setback. Tony and the lads in the club sat in their seats and kept their heads down. I got out of the van and the lads in the hides had joined me on a side street; we would stay there in case things kicked off. Tony had got Jock and Platty to head over to the bar ready to cause a scene if it looked like David had spotted Tony, but lucky for us he didn't. The lads made their way out of the club just to be on the safe side.

When the lad arrived out of the club, they made their way around to the side street to meet up with the rest of us. Dunc thought we should wait until they came back out of the club and then grab them. As we'd had nothing in three weeks, we would be pulled off the job soon, so this would probably be our only chance of getting somewhere. Donny, Brit and Platty didn't agree. They thought it was too risky and could blow the whole operation.

"No, I think it'll work," I said. "Back in Good Brewers David was about to tell me about the doormen that drink in their pub, but Rob his mate stopped him two or three times. I think it'll work, and if it doesn't, we can hold them until we get a break or we contact BSM Bob.

Smeet, Donny, Evo and Chris agreed. It had been decided, we would wait until they came back out. As we had three of the cars with us, we would follow them and hopefully get them on their way home. Me, Chris and Jock in the back car, Brit, Tony and Evo in the middle car, and Platty, Dunc and Donny in the front car; the rest would follow at a distance in the van.

Duncan Bustin

(Dunc)

Royal Artillery, 1979 to 2001

We all got in the cars at the ready, and stayed out of the way. I headed down to the main road and waited in a side street ready to join the tailing; the second car waited at the side of the club, and the lead car headed down to the roundabout on the main road. As they had to head that way, there was no other way out of the village apart from the way we lived, and that would only end up in the sea. The van did the observation at the club just waiting to give us the go. We sat for about two hours just waiting, then it happened – out they came.

This time there were three of them that got in the car. One was the lad Evo had been working with. *What the hell was he doing?* Smeet contacted us all to follow but stay back, we couldn't take the chance of a local lad going missing.

As the car passed me I got ready to join in the tailing, and when Evo's car passed I set off. I noticed the van had also set off, sitting back from us. As we got to the roundabout we could see Donny's car. I held back to allow Donny in. This was it, we had started on the tailing, my first ever. But this was not like you see on the TV – we really did have to be careful.

As we drove along the road, we would keep changing puissance in the tailing, so as not to raise suspicion. We followed them for about fifteen minutes before they turned off into a hotel car park. The front two cars drove past, the van stopped short of the hotel, and my car stopped on the street opposite. Keeping our heads down, we observed.

All three got out of the car and stood chatting, it looked like the 'thread' man was just showing them the way to the hotel, and could be waiting for a lift back to the club. It was decided that the van and one car would head home and my car and Platty's would stay and observe. It only took about ten minutes before we were proven right. In came a car and the lad jumped in, but David and his mate, whose name I still couldn't remember, just stood at the doors of the hotel. Then David opened the boot of the car and picked up the bags and headed into the hotel, while his mate stood outside.

Donny thought the same as Platty, they would be going for a late night stroll. I didn't think so, but I was wrong. David came out and off they set. They headed down a track at the side of the hotel into a wooded area, and that was the chance we needed. Five of us followed, and left Platty with the cars. If we needed a car, he could bring it as close to the track as possible.

The track led to a canal out of the earshot of any houses, so this was probably the best chance we would get. Four of us got into the thicket, two either side of the track, and Chris followed them down the track to report back to us if anything was going on. They might have been going to meet up with someone, Big Bob would be ideal. We knew Chris wouldn't be recognised as he hadn't been seen with us in the past. David and his mate must have walked about 800 yards or so down the canal bank before they turned around. At this point, Chris got on the radio and informed us he wouldn't turn back so not to raise suspicion. As he walked past them, he nodded his head as if to say good evening, and they both acknowledged with a good evening. Chris walked on about another 30 yards and turned to check. They were now out of sight, so he headed back towards us making sure he kept out of sight. We prepared to jump them.

The first thing we would have to do was to keep them quiet. As they approached I could feel the sweat running down my back, my throat was dry and my head was back in the Yorkshire moors, remembering what I had felt like when I was being hunted down. Although David and his mate weren't aware we were there, I still felt for them. It had nothing to do with them, but they could help we all hoped. We let them pass me and Jock and then we jumped them from behind. As we did, Donny and Tony came in from the front and both planted a punch to the face simultaneously. Before I could grab him, down he went. I still followed his head as he hit the floor to stop him calling out. We covered their mouths and dragged them into the side of the track. That was enough to scare them, although Jock did have a knife to David's mate's throat. I grabbed a small torch out of my pocket and shone it directly in the face of David.

"If you cooperate you won't be hurt, do you understand?"

He stopped wriggling and his mate did the same. He stared at me as if to say, *what the hell is happening?*, then his gaze changed, he'd recognised me, not believing what I was doing in Wales never mind jumping him and his mate.

"We are going to take our hands off your mouths, but one word and you'll be sorry. We don't want to hurt you but we will if we have to." I looked at Dunc. He had replaced me with his hand over David's mouth, and now he slowly released it.

"What's going on John?" he asked in a soft voice.

"I'm not who you think I am, we need to speak with you both in private, do you understand?" He nodded and looked at his mate. His mate did the same, he nodded. As Jock slowly removed the knife from his throat, he also released his hand from his mouth.

"OK lads, get up, and no funny business," Chris said as

he rejoined us.

David was first to his feet. "I don't understand why you're doing this John." You could see he was scared.

"We'll explain it all to you later." As his mate got to his feet I asked him his name. "Ant, right, you're the owner of the club aren't you?"

"Yes," he said, "and if it's money you want I have plenty, you can have it."

"No, mate, it's not money, and we aren't going to hurt you either if you cooperate." Tony handed Ant a hanky to wipe the blood from his face.

"Then what do you want with us?" he said as he wiped the blood.

"Information, nothing more at the moment, so let us go back to your hotel and have a chat. If either one of you tries to do anything, *WE'LL KILL YOU!*" That was the first time I had ever said those words and meant it.

Jock had always wanted to kill someone, and I think he would without a second thought. He had joined the army for that one purpose, and we all could tell he loved the thought of killing someone, that was a good thing. We all had the same in us: if it came to it, we would kill, and some of us had in the past, not that we'd wanted to but we had too, as the saying goes *them or you.*

As we got back to the end of the track, Platty had the car waiting. Chris thought it best we keep one of them in the car and head to the hotel with the one. "Yes, let's do that," I agreed, looking at David. "You come with me to the hotel and Ant will sit in the car with Platty and Jock."

Me and Chris headed to the hotel with David. We walked one either side of him, just in case he tried to run. I didn't think he would but you can never be sure. As we walked I noticed the van at the end of the road with Smeet in the driving seat. Donny had also noticed it, and changed the plan. He, Dunc and Tony walked Ant to the van and thought they could get him to talk as well. It's always best if you need information off two or more, you always separate them. So that's what happened and it worked. We had a good feeling that they wouldn't be involved, and it turned out they weren't, but David *did* know a bit about what had been going on, but was too scared to say anything or get involved.

When we got to the hotel the young lady behind the reception desk asked if we were all booking in. David had only booked for him and Ant, but as she hadn't seen Ant one of us could get in as him. Chris piped up, "No love, I'm hoping to just have a drink with my mates."

"OK," she said, "just don't let anyone in the bar now as it's supposed to be residents only."

Chris thanked her as we passed the desk. I pushed David towards a table in the corner away from the one table that was occupied. I sat with my back to the wall, while Chris sat next to David facing me.

"OK David, let's get one thing straight, DON'T try and fob us off with any shit … you be straight with us and things will be good for you." This was not the sort of kid that gets himself into shit like this; you could see he was shitting it. The best approach we could do was to be nice to him, put him at ease and things would normally go well.

It worked. David told us all about the paintings, they had brought one with them today. He said it had to have the blood dripping from the eye again – that could only mean one thing, that there was going to be a hunt and soon. According

– 142 –

to David the painting had to be down here no later than next Friday, that was all he really knew, and he didn't have a clue about any of it. So we got them together after telling them about what had been going on and from his clubs. We also informed them about what had happened to me, Brit and Kenny. Ant wasn't happy that it had been conducted from his clubs, but they both agreed to help us, and assured us they would get whatever we needed if they could. We didn't want them to get too involved as we wouldn't be able to protect them if the doormen got suspicious. One thing I asked them to drop in a conversation was that Big Bob had gone missing.

Ant asked if that was Bob the head doorman at his club in Lincolnshire. We said we thought so, that we only knew him as Bob. Apparently, he'd gone missing with a lot more of the lads that worked the doors. "Don't worry about the rest, we just need Big Bob," we said. "We know he is in the area but we don't know where, so if you can just try and drop it in one of your conversations with the lads back at the club." They agreed to. At last we seemed to be getting somewhere, and we were happy to let them go for now.

"But remember one thing lads," I said, "*DON'T* try anything stupid or you will be very sorry, and your pub back in Scunthorpe will be gone in no time."

We agreed that they would be met each night, at a different location and time for updates. We would give them the location and time the night before. We didn't want them to ring us, just in case the phones got tapped. We let them go and assured them if things went well and we got what we needed, they would be fine. Ant was well pissed off with David; he felt let down by him not telling him about the paintings, but to be fair, he was scared shitless of the doormen – or that's what it seemed like to me.

The next day we all got up early, it seemed that we all felt the same, there was a good vibe about this. When I opened the curtains, it was a bright sunny day for the time of year, the sky was clear and the sun was shining through the bare branches of the trees outside the house.

Paul Donoghue

(Donny)

Royal Artillery, 1977 to 1984

THE END OF IT ALL
(possibly)

Tony and Scouse were in the kitchen with Evo getting breakfast ready. When I looked along the street, I could see Kenny and Glenn heading off for a run. Chris was sitting on the wall having a smoke, which was more his style; he was quite a fit lad but would rather have a smoke or a pint than go for a run. As we sat down to breakfast Evo asked what we would be doing that day, it was Friday and we still had to go to work, or at least some of us did. Tony and Scouse would be meeting up with the rest of the lads that were lucky enough not to have work; they would go through things from the night before, and set up plans for the night ahead. We couldn't wait, the thought of getting the chance to have something happen and information on Big Bob had us all on a high.

After work me and Kenny walked home with a spring in our steps, we didn't say a lot but I could tell he was in a good place – as I was. When I arrived at the house Tony and Scouse had the map on the table ready to go through the plan for the night. I headed upstairs for a bath, so they would have to wait (I wasn't going out again smelling like a down and out again) and I would have to be given one of the better jobs, *not* in a hide. Kenny wasn't bothered what job he got as long as he was on the job, but he wasn't in the house with us, so I presumed Glenn would be doing the same with him. The rest of the lads had been through it all earlier in the day. There was me, Evo and Smeet. Scouse hadn't gone to work that morning, he had phoned in sick. There was nothing wrong with him, just his mind was on the job for the evening and he couldn't get it out of his head.

After I had showered and had tea, Tony and Scouse went

through it all with us. Evo was to change the signs on the van halfway down the road; Chris and Brit would help him. Smeet and Jock would also be in the van. I would have one car with Dunc and Glenn, and I was happy with that. I enjoyed working with the two of them, for some reason I felt confident with them around. In car two would be Platty, Donny and Tony, and in the third car would be the final two – Scouse and Kenny. Again we all had wires on. The van had coms with camp, but this time BSM Bob and Ian would be on the other end.

We all got into position. Jock, Evo and Platty headed for the club as arranged, Brit got the hide and me and Glenn got to walk the streets with Dunc. Something was going to happen that night, I could feel it in my water.

The van was parked over the road from the club and my team would keep walking past every hour. At times we would swap over with three of the lads in the van. Smeet had been in contact with BSM Bob and he wanted more in the club, so Chris and Smeet headed in and sat away from the rest of the lads.

The club was starting to fill up, there were quite a few minibuses pulling up, and it looked like they were lads and lassies from out of town. This could be what the doormen had been waiting for. We also noticed that there were a lot more doormen on duty that night.

Time had started to get on, when Ant and David arrived in the same car as the previous evening, an Audi 80 *(what a car! Something I couldn't afford at that time of my life)*. As they got out of the car they were met by two of the doormen, who seemed to rush out to meet them (something to hide, we thought). Just as Ant and David were being rushed into the club a second car arrived. Three big, hard looking men got out and just stood looking around. That was until a third car turned up. Bingo! Big Bob was in the third car.

I was in the van at the time he arrived, and I could feel the hairs on my arms stand up, and a cold shiver down my spine. At the same time the sweat ran down my whole body and my eyes started to sting as it crept in at the sides.

"THAT'S HIM," I said, *"that's the bastard that got me outside the shed."* That was a face I wouldn't forget as long as I lived.

At the time Tony had been sitting at the back of the van having a cuppa. He jumped up immediately and confirmed it was Big Bob. I looked at him, my face burning with rage and I could see that same rage in his face. We both turned and looked at Kenny. He was so calm I couldn't understand him. He looked at me and said quietly, "Don't worry lads, he's here ... and we *will* get him this time." This was not the Kenny we knew; he had changed to become a calm and patient man, and to be fair he had – we just hadn't noticed it until that moment.

As Big Bob got out of the car the big lads that had just got out of the other car went straight over to escort him (or so it appeared to us) into the club. As Dunc got on to camp, Kenny got on to the lads in the club, informing them that Big Bob was on his way in. He also gave a description of what Big Bob was wearing. Smeet and Chris got up from the table they had been sitting at and headed towards a better viewing point within the club. Evo and his lads stayed put in the corner as it was a good view point anyway. We were all starting to get a bit on edge. We were certain something was going to happen – and not before time as far as I was concerned.

We got reports back from Platty. Ant and David had gone into a room at the back of the club, and that was where Big Bob and *the big lads* (as we now referred to them) had gone as well. This was the time we would find out if Ant and David valued their business and their lives. This time we really didn't have anyone on the inside, not like when Donny got in back at Lincolnshire. He had been a great help and if it hadn't been for him getting in Brit, Kenny and me might not be there now.

Jock contacted the van with an update. Ant and one of the big lads had come out of the room and were headed towards a door at the side of the bar. Jock joined the queue and hoped he would still be in it as they came back out as he hadn't got a good look at Big Bob prior to him going in, and he hadn't come across him the last time on the hunt. But before he had the chance, the big lads and David all came out of the room at the back of the club, and one of them appeared to have the painting under his arm. Chris got on the wire to inform us. Glenn and Dunc then headed for the cars and sat at the ready, waiting to head down towards the club to pick up the lads in case they needed to follow them on them leaving the club.

Evo was checking on the door by the bar, and out came Ant and Big Bob. They met up with the rest of the lads, shook hands, and Ant and David left. Glenn headed down towards the club and picked me up, so we could catch up with them as agreed. Off we went, keeping two cars between us.

Back at the club the big lads came outside and stood chatting with the two lads on the door; it was clear one of them was not happy about something as he waved his arms and then stormed off. One of the big lads headed after him, pushed him against the wall, and appeared to have stern words with him. It seemed to us that he'd given in to whatever had been said, as he held his arms up in a gesture as if to say *OK you win*. They then walked back to the rest of the lads with the big lad's arm around his shoulder. You could still see the lad off the door was still not happy about whatever had been said earlier. *He* was one we needed to get to and hopefully we'd get information off him.

Chris and Smeet had been called to leave the club and get the third car, park it closer to the club and keep an eye on the doorman that wasn't happy. They had to follow him and apprehend him, as we all thought he had to have information on whatever was going on. By this time me and Dunc had met up with Ant and David.

Ant wasn't happy, as the man that he thought was running the club wasn't; it seemed to be the big lads. The lad that should be running it was working behind the bar, so it seemed that they had taken over the club. He was still getting profit from the club but something wasn't right, but not being a confrontational sort he didn't want to start anything with them.

It turned out that the so called manager was too scared to do or say anything, and the club had been run by the big lads for some time. But Ant didn't have a clue on what to do. How could he get it back in the hands of his manager, or someone that wasn't scared of the big lads? I knew only too well that desperate feeling, it is the worst feeling in the world – no one to turn to or ask for help – so I made a deal with him. "If you go along with everything we do and say, we'll get the club back for you."

Ant looked at David and thankfully David nodded. Good, we were getting somewhere.

When they were back at the club, Ant wanted to know what had happened to the lads that had worked the doors for him back at Lincolnshire. Big Bob said they'd gone out on the drink one night and they'd got into a fight, but no one had seen them for weeks and he'd had family members around asking questions.

"I thought you would have let me know."

"Sorry mate," Big Bob said, "but I came down here to see my mates, and didn't know anything about it until I phoned the wife." That was a load of shit, he knew *exactly* what was going on. David said they had come to the club to pick up the painting. I asked what it was for but all I got was it was for a competition some of his lads were doing the following weekend. This was a big help, not that David would understand it, but we had a lead – the following weekend.

So now we had to keep a close eye on Big Bob and the big lads. This wasn't going to be easy. The main two we would have to follow was Big Bob and the leader of the rest. But who was he? However, it turned out to be much easier than we had first thought.

As Evo was walking out of the club with Platty he was stopped by the lad he had been working with over the last few weeks.

"Hi Andy, I didn't know you were in the club mate."

"Yes, we've been in for a couple of hours now."

"This is my Dad I was telling you about," and he pointed to the biggest one of the *big lads*.

Evo stuck his hand out as if to shake his, but he just got a nod at first then out came a hand like a shovel.

Andy grabbed it the best he could, his finger ends just about covered the palm and he thought to himself, *if that hits you, you would know all about it.* "I'm Andy Johnson."

Platty looked at him as if to say, *you're* not Johnson, but then realised why he had said it.

"And *you* are?" just waiting for the reply, *Paul.*

"Paul Wilson, good to meet you. My lad said he worked with some lads that had come down here looking for work, so where are you from originally?"

Evo didn't want to say his home town, if anything went wrong he didn't want them looking for him in the place he grew up, so he said on the outskirts of Hull, he could get away with that as he had been up there working with the army on his advanced driving course. So *this* was the leader. We now had a face and a name. Evo and Platty said their goodbyes and off they went.

Brit was still in his hide. He had seen the big lad (we now knew to be Paul) grab the doorman that was not happy about something, and had got on the radio asking if we had seen the same. We had.

"We need to get him at the end of the night lads," Brit said.

I didn't get the whole conversation but there was a mention of getting a young lad for the weekend. Brit was a lot closer to the club than we were. Brit was asked if he would be able to get out of the hide without being seen or heard. He replied he could. "Then make your way around to the side street, and you'll be picked up."

Brit got himself out of the hide and onto the street, where he was met by Evo, Platty and Donny, with a car. Their job was to follow the doorman when he finished his shift on the door. The rest of the lads stayed in the van looking over the club doorway. By that time, Me and Dunc had finished with Ant and David. We had been instructed to head back to the house, but that wasn't going to happen. We knew there was going to be action that night and we had no intention of missing out on it. We knew the side street that Brit had been sent to, so we headed there.

Sitting just around the corner from Brit and the lads, we would wait until they set off and then follow them.

Glenn had been hanging around outside the club, but Tony and Kenny had thought it was time he headed back to the van. As he started to walk away a fight started outside the club doors. All the doormen joined in, except the one that hadn't been happy earlier. Glenn stood back and watched. Kenny was on the radio for him to get out of the way, but Glenn took no notice. He sat on a wall just watched.

It didn't take long for things to settle down, but Glenn hadn't been watching the fight as we'd thought, he'd been watching the doormen and the big lads, to see which ones were the fighters. Glenn always studied fights, always trying to work out the best way to beat someone.

After the club closed and the doormen started to leave, the intention was to follow the doorman that was upset; we had also found out his name – Mal. At least, *that* had been the intention, to find out his address so we could pay him a visit one day to get information out of him. As the doormen started to leave something happened that we didn't expect. Paul (the leader, we thought) was telling Mal to get into his car with two more of the doormen. Mal wasn't happy but it seemed that he had no choice; it looked as if they had the intention of giving him a good hiding. As they left Tony got on the radio, instructing Platty to head off after them, but to keep a good distance behind so as not to be seen.

Me and Dunc did the same. As Dunc drove off I had a thought: all the cars we had had been fitted with tracers and all the cars could track each other, so I switched it on and bingo, we picked Platty's car up straight away. That meant we could keep out of sight and still follow them.

We drove for about four miles before they turned into an estate. We switched off the headlights, and slowly made our way in. When we got a sighting of Platty's car we stopped, keeping our heads down. We stayed in the car for about five minutes, when Dunc suggested if we got out and headed on foot we might see where Paul had pulled up.

The street was a long and winding road, with plenty of cars and vans dotted along it. The street lighting was dim and there wasn't a house light on that we could see. Platty and the lads had stayed in their car with their heads down. Me and Dunc continued to walk slowly along the street, making sure we kept out of sight of Platty's and Paul's car. We got a sighting of Paul's car, the lights on and the engine running. We managed to get past Platty's car without being seen. We had to have been about 25 yards off Paul's car, hiding behind a van, when I noticed a garden that was full of hedging. I tapped Dunc on the shoulder and we made our way into it – that gave us more cover and got us a lot closer.

Suddenly, the passenger car door opened, and out got Mal. As he stood by the door with his head looking back into the car, he said goodnight and seemed a lot happier than he had been when he got into it. He banged the door shut and made his way into a gate on the opposite side of the street. He put his key in the door and looked back at the car as it pulled away. The plan was to just find out the address and pay him a visit later on in the week, but Dunc thought differently; he thought we should go in now. It was dark quiet and if there was anyone else in the house they would probably be in bed. *Yes, why not?* I thought, we still had our radios on, so I called out, "We're going in." We could see the lads in the car with Platty, their heads all popped up at the same time. Glenn was back with Tony and Kenny.

"NO! NO! NO!" he called out over the radio. We knew why. He wanted some of the action himself. Sorry mate, we're going in.

Evo was looking all around to see where we were.

We walked out of the garden and gave him a wave. Jumping out of the car first, Evo ran over to us.

"WHAT ARE YOU DOING?"

We explained, that if we went in now we could catch him off guard and if he didn't want to be part of it, he could *go missing* and Paul would think he had done a runner. Evo agreed it made sense, so I briefed the lads. I would knock on the door and he would open it most probably thinking it would be his mates calling back to tell him something that they had forgotten to tell him in the car on the way home.

Dunc passed the car keys over to Brit. "You drive when we come back out with him mate."

I set up the snatch.

The house was a semi-detached so I got Donny and Platty to wait at the back door just in case he tried to do a runner. Evo was down the side of the house keeping a check on a window on the ground floor. Me, Brit and Dunc were at the front door. The door was a full wooden one without any windows, nor did it have a spyhole. I took a deep breath, looked at Brit and Dunc – they both gave me a small nod as if to say *we're ready* – I turned to the door … and gave it one loud three rap knock and stood ready to dive in. I looked at the living room window; the curtain flickered from the breeze of the living room door opening. I heard the lock on the front door turn. It had opened no more than an inch when I rammed it with my shoulder. The door smashed against the man inside, knocking him back into the living room. Before I had a chance to regain my balance, I was pushed from behind and knocked to the floor.

Brit and Dunc had forced themselves past me. By the time I got back to my feet the man was on the floor, with Brit and Dunc on top of him. The man was calling out for help and Brit went to gag him – but my foot got to his head first. The feeling wasn't good as I knew he didn't want to be part of the hunt, but I couldn't be soft on him now, he had to know we meant business. Dunc and Brit dragged him to his feet; he was semi-conscious and now moaning more than shouting. At this point, Evo, Donny and Platty ran in, slamming the door behind them.

As Brit and Dunc continued to hold him upright, I brought my foot up and gave him a mawashi geri to the side of the head, just soft enough *not* to knock him unconscious, but hard enough to let him know we meant business. Donny got a chair from the dining table in the corner of the room, and put it in the middle of the room. Dunc and Brit slumped him down onto it and Platty and Evo strapped him down. As I stood in front of him, he lifted his head slowly and looked dazedly up at me. I didn't give him the chance to say a word. When my fist smashed against his nose, the sound of the bone snapping gave Evo and Platty a shock, they had never been in a situation like this before (well, Platty had, but he hadn't thought we would be doing this to him). All we needed was information, but to get it and get it quick we had to be rough. I stood behind him, put my hand on the top of his head and asked him the question:

"What is the plan for the hunt?"

"I...don't know...what...you mean," was his reply.

That was the wrong answer.

I put my fingers up his nose and ripped his head back over. Brit covered his mouth as he was about to scream out. As I held his head back, Dunc started snapping his fingers one at a time. As the first one snapped, the pain flared in his eyes – they opened wide and a watery glaze came over them. They looked like clear blue marbles with fiery red streaks. The screams leaked out from his gag and hot tears rolled down his cheeks.

As his body began to settle slightly, I slowly released his head. Dunc let go of his hands and Brit slowly removed his hand from Mal's mouth.

"Now you need to *talk* ... that is, if you value your life," Dunc told him.

Evo is a soft spoken man and thought he would try and encourage him to speak before we started again (sort of good cop, bad cop routine). Mal could hardly utter a word as he was trying to hold back the tears. Evo knew, like we all did, that Mal didn't want anything to do with the hunt, but that was no interest to us. All we needed was information, and Mal was the one to give it.

One more finger snapped, and one direct punch to the

side of the head and he squealed like a baby, telling us everything.

There was going to be a hunt, and Big Bob would be there. We all thought it would be in the Wales area, but no, it was going to be on Dartmoor, very much like the Yorkshire moors. Once again a cold shiver ran through my whole body, remembering what I had been through with two of my best mates. And this was probably only one young lad, that had no experience in survival or anything like it. Now we needed to get Mal out of his house and get him to a safe place. Would it be to the houses we had or somewhere else? That wasn't my call, so for now it would have to be the houses we had. The lads got the cars at the ready while me, Evo and Brit headed up the stairs to have a look around.

In the corner of the back bedroom were two suitcases. We grabbed them, lay them on the bed, and started to fill them with clothes out of the wardrobe and drawers. We deliberately left some lying on the floor and bed, so it would look like he had done a runner. Big Bob and the rest would go for it, as it was known he didn't want to be part of the hunt. One thing we didn't get out of him was where exactly on the moors the hunt was to take place. Someone, somewhere knew it and would have a map or instructions on how to get there.

We double-checked that the street was all clear before we bundled Mal into the boot of one of the cars, we then checked the house again to ensure we hadn't left anything behind. We were satisfied that it looked as if Mal had done a runner. Then we left.

As we drove, Platty got on the net to inform Tony at the control van what we now had, and what we now knew.

We needed advice on what to do with Mal as we knew we wouldn't be able to keep him in the houses we had, at least not for long, as that would drop the numbers of men we had. It would be a 24-hour job looking after him.

Tony, Glenn and Kenny weren't happy that me and Dunc had changed the plans; it was never a good thing to change plans in mid flow, but this time we had decided it was the right thing to do (and it did, in fact, turn out to be the case). However, Tony wouldn't see that, more because I knew all three of them couldn't wait for action, and we had just had a bit of it without them.

Time was getting on. 03:12hours and we had arrived back at the house. Smeet came out to meet us, wanting to know what car he was in. "This one," I informed him. He then jumped in the back with Dunc, and informed Brit to turn around and head back to town. I couldn't think what was happening.

"We have to take him to a camp called Brawdy."

I hadn't heard of it, but learnt it was an RAF camp on the coastal road not far from St David. It took us about forty minutes. As we headed along the coast road we got a call from Chris on the net that we would see two Land Rovers parked on the side of the coast road, about a mile from the camp. We had to put our balaclavas on, as we couldn't be seen by military personnel.

When we arrived, five RAF lads were standing alongside the Land Rovers. I got out of the car and walked towards them. A sergeant walked towards me, calling out, "Are you Geordie?"

"Yes," I replied.

"You have something for me," he said.

"Yes, but you need to reverse the Land Rover up to the back of the car."

He turned and indicated to his lads with the wave of one hand. They jumped into the Rovers, one turned his Rover to block the lay-by entrance, the other reversed his up to the back of the car. You could see they hadn't a clue what was going on, as the excitement on their faces said an exercise that was different to the norm. So, the man in the boot was to them a soldier playing the part of a prisoner. The sergeant would be the only one that had been informed that he was not a soldier, but that would be all.

They dropped the tailgate. As we opened the boot, we had a bag over Mal's head so the damage to his face wouldn't be seen. It turned out that the camp had a cell in the guard room that could only be accessed from the back, and it had not been used for years. We dragged Mal out of the boot, and weren't gentle. The young soldiers were shocked at how rough we were with him. As they lifted the tailgate, two of them jumped in with him, the sergeant and one other. That was it. We all got back into the car and headed back to the house. And that was the last we saw of Mal. I did feel a bit sorry for him, but if you mix in that kind of circle you have to be prepared for the worst.

One thing I'd noticed about all of this hunt game was that there were no Geordies involved in any of them. I did know a few doormen from up north, some I had gone to school with. They had bigger fish to fry; picking on defenceless young lads wasn't their game. Taking over another area and fighting the so called *hard* men, that's what they thrived on. A bit of fun for the Geordie doormen was to fight big, hard men – you win and you get your name, you lose and you try again, until you feel enough is enough and give up, and go back to a *normal life* as they call it.

When we arrived back at the houses, the place was in darkness. The lads had all hit the sack, so we got away with an ear-bashing from Tony, Glenn and Kenny – at least until the morning.

The next day we all sat around the table in the middle house, to get an update on the situation. To our surprise Mal had spoken up to the RAF sergeant and had given him the address where Big Bob was. This was brilliant, he was staying with the top man around these parts, Paul Wilson. When Evo heard the name he piped up, "I've met him."

We all looked at him and demanded to know when and where.

"At the club last night, I'm working with his son and he introduced him to me last night ... he is big, *very* big."

So, now we knew where he lived we'd have to stake out the house. The instructions came from BSM Wilson, so Tony, Glenn, Smeet and Chris, would be on the stakeout. That would require a recky of the area. We decided to send Dunc, Jock and Platty to do the recky.

"Evo, you're to keep working and get as close as you can to Paul's son, and find out anything you can about his dad."

"Billy is his name," Evo said.

The rest of us had to just get on and continue doing what we had been doing – working or looking for work – but we had to keep out of trouble. After the meeting we all headed off to do our thing.

Me and Kenny headed off to the fish quay, while Brit, Donny and Jock headed upstairs to sort out the equipment. Glenn would double-check that everything worked and everything was there (the *last* thing you need is equipment that is U/S when you deploy in a hide. Glenn also had equipment of his own that he would get out, and in time let us have, but he would have to go through everything with us carefully, as some of the equipment none of us had used before.

Later that day me and Kenny sat down to dinner on the side of the fish quay. It was a fresh autumn day and the sun was low in the fresh clear sky. The sound of the ripples from a passing boat slapping against the side of the harbour was so relaxing, it made me feel good about myself, and I was so excited that we had eventually got to the stage where action was going to happen. We had been through hell on the Yorkshire moors, and now we had the chance to get revenge. The only three of the group that had been on the receiving end of a hunt was me, Kenny and Brit, but now we had a chance to have action from the other side – being a hunter instead of the hunted.

Jock, Platty and Dunc had been sent out to do a recky of the area around the house Big Bob was staying at. They drove to a nearby pub and parked the car, headed to a shop over the road, so as not to arouse suspicions. After they'd left the shop they headed up the street and then split up. Dunc was to try and get around the back of the house, Jock and Platty the front. Platty and Jock turned left onto the street where the house was – it was a private estate with twelve houses, all detached and very expensive looking.

All the gardens had well-kept lawns and lovely flower beds, except two. One was two doors down from the house we had to recky (that was Paul's house), and the other, to our advantage, was over the road from it. The both of them had large overgrown areas. The house over the road had a willow tree and its branches hung down to the ground. The leaves hadn't fallen from the tree yet, but it wouldn't be long, maybe two weeks at the most, Jock thought. It would be hard for the one that got picked for that one, as he would probably have to sit up. The other garden was different, it was bracken, so someone could lie down under it. Both gardens had small picket fences, so there was great vision to the house and a good part of the street.

Jock and Platty walked the street three times just to get it right. As they walked it for the last time, Platty stepped into a gateway. An old man was standing at a window looking out at them. By the time Platty had approached the door, the old man had already opened it. Platty asked if he'd heard of a man called Taff Jones (pretty stupid really, as in Wales half of the men are probably called Jones and known as Taff or Taffy). Jock sniggered as he looked on. The old man just said no and shut the door in Platty's face. When he turned to look at Jock, Jock's snigger had turned into a full laugh. Once Jock started laughing you couldn't stop him.

They headed back towards the car, while Dunc was still checking out the back garden. As luck would have it, Dunc had found that a wood lay behind the garden. It was a thick dense one with a lot of growth under the trees, so it was ideal for a hideout. When Dunc returned to the car, Jock and Platty had already started to sketch out the area, showing the gardens and the street.

Back at our houses Glenn was putting all the equipment together for the hides. We had put Glenn in charge because tech was one of his strong points. On occasion we had to ask what some of the items were – there were things we hadn't seen before, and many items we'd been given were not standard issue for a normal soldier.

Evo was a godsend, working with Billy (who wasn't the brightest of lad). Billy gave Evo everything we needed, most of it came about through bragging about what his dad had done and what he was doing now. A key thing he revealed was that his dad was going away for a week with his mates, on a holiday he said, but Evo knew different. He knew that Dartmoor was the place, but we couldn't understand why at the time.

Dunc and the lads arrived back at the house. Jock headed to the kitchen to pop the kettle on, while Dunc and Platty cleared the dining table. They laid down a large sheet of paper ready to start sketching the layout of the area for the stakeout. Brit, Smeet and Chris had been upstairs with Glenn sorting out the equipment. By this time me and Kenny had finished work and were heading home. We assumed Evo was still at work, but he had headed out for a drink with some of the lads from work. Billy was one of them. For me this was a good thing, as it meant a chance to get in with him more. The rest of the lads had gone to the house next door to chill out.

Once Dunc had the area layout completed on paper, and Glenn had all the equipment laid out, we just had to wait for Evo to get home. We would then all go through it together, and any questions and answers heard by all. However, Evo was off his face when he got back, so we had to put him to bed and sort him out in the morning. Smeet and Tony weren't happy. We'd all agreed that yes, we could have a drink, but in moderation – the one thing we *didn't* want to happen, was one of us getting into trouble with the police or any of the locals.

The next day, as I was setting up for breakfast, Evo came downstairs with Chris and Smeet. I could hear them giving Evo a telling off about the state he was in. Evo thought it was funny. I don't know what happened, but I saw red. As he walked through the dining room doors, I smashed him one right in the face, then I grabbed him and threw him against the wall. Smeet and Chris grabbed me and tried to pull me off him. Meanwhile, Donny had heard the commotion and came rushing down the stairs. He pushed through Smeet and Chris, grabbed me by the head and dragged me into the living room out of the way. I was raging. Evo had jeopardised the whole thing. I tried to explain to Donny that the chance to get revenge on that lot meant everything to me. First, to get them back for what they'd done to Kenny, Brit and me, and second, we had to think of the young kids out there, that had no chance of defending themselves. It started to dawn on Evo what he had done – I knew he would never have done it on purpose – and he came in to apologise to me. I could see he meant it, Evo didn't have a bad bone in his body. I got up (well, once Donny had got off the top of me) and gave Evo a hug … and that was that, put to bed. That's the thing with the army lads, once a disagreement is over, that's the end of it.

We all cracked on with breakfast and running through who was doing what. Tony and the rest of the lads came in from the other houses, so before everyone got on with their jobs, Glenn went through everything again, just for Evo's benefit. Tony and Brit had changed things again, this was the norm with the regiment, you would be given a task, and be briefed on all others, and at the last minute it would change. This was in case we had been compromised and you were a target. So, it had been decided that four would be in the hides, Donny and Jock would be at the back of the house, Dunc would be in the garden over the road from Paul's house, and Chris would be in the one down the street. After that day we would have only four days left until things started to move. The nights had started to draw in, and the cold winds had picked up, so it was essential they had all the equipment necessary for the job and the cold weather (it is surprising how many soldiers forget equipment and suffer for it).

We always worked together and would check each other's kit. Once everyone knew what was to happen that night, we went about the day as normal; we thought we were getting somewhere at last, morale was high and you could feel the excitement in the group. I headed off to the fish quay with Kenny and all we spoke about was what we would do to the hunters when we caught up with them.

That night the lads went off in the cars with Platty and Smeet. They had to ensure the coast was clear before dropping them off. Donny and Jock weren't a problem, as they got dropped at the woods, but Dunc and Chris had to walk the streets for a while. After about an hour and a half Smeet started to get coms from them; Dunc was in place, Chris had a bit trouble getting into position as it was tight in the bracken, Donny and Jock had no problem at all, they had a perfect view of the house and as luck would have it, the living room had patio doors to it, with Venetian blinds.

The only thing we didn't like about being in a hide was,

once you got in you *stayed* in; the toilet was an old bottle and a plastic bag.

The first night was reasonably quiet. Paul and his wife (we think she was) had tea at the table in the window area, and after that Paul headed out for the night. His wife headed to the kitchen, did the dishes and then settled down for the night in front of the TV, the only time she moved was to make a cuppa or to switch the TV over.

Evo had decided to go for another drink with Billy, but this time he made sure he didn't get drunk. The good news from that was he had been invited to Billy's house for tea on Thursday night, the night before they would be heading off to Dartmoor.

Time was getting on, and Dunc and Chris had not seen much. At about 01:00 hours Paul pulled up in his car with one other man. They both got out and headed indoors. Dunc got on the radio to Jock to inform him. The blinds had been left open all night so Donny and Jock had a great view. Nothing happened. They just sat at the table counting money (and there was a lot of it!). Jock reported back to Smeet, and that was about it. The second night was much the same, and night three was the changeover night. To my surprise, me and Brit had been picked to do the hide at the back of the house, Kenny and Glenn got the front. The job we had at the fish quay, we just didn't go back to. We did feel sorry for the owner but we couldn't say anything, the job we had come down here to do was about to start – and that was the only thing that mattered to us.

The first night in the hide was pretty much the same as the last two had been, nothing to report as such. On the night Evo was going for tea was a different thing all together. We had told Evo to get any information he could, have a look around the house if he got the chance, but one thing we didn't want, was for him to get caught. Kenny got on the net, a car had pulled up outside the house, with two men in it. Soon after a second car rolled up, this time it was Evo and Billy. When Billy got out, two of the men in the other car got out to shake his hand. As Evo got out one of the men asked who he was. "This is my mate I work with," Billy said.

"Nice boy," the man said, "just my type" and he laughed.

Evo didn't find this funny, but he smiled just to keep the peace. Paul came out the house and climbed into the front seat, opened the window and said to Billy "You out tonight son?"

"Yes," was his reply, "we're having tea with Mam, and then heading to the club."

"See you there son," Paul said.

Evo thought this was good as he only had to worry about Billy and his mam now. Billy's dad set off with his mates to the club, and Billy and Evo headed into the house. As they did so, Glenn could see Evo looking around, as if to say *where the hell are you?* Things went quiet again. Me and Brit could see them sitting down to tea. *Twat* we thought, Evo having a slap up meal, and there was us, army ration packs, cold beans and ham.

The three of them sat at the table for about an hour, then Billy got up and headed upstairs. The back bedroom light went on and then the bathroom light. Billy was having a shower. Evo asked if it was OK to go up to the toilet, and was told it was next to the bathroom. Evo thought it would be a good chance to have a look around.

He had a look in the front room (that was Paul's and his

wife's). There was a safe in the corner, a notebook on top of it. A quick look through it, it was all cash figures, and a lot by all accounts. Evo got out and went into Billy's room. He stood at the window (he knew me and Brit would be looking up at him) and started making signs to indicate a lot of cash in the house, twisting his hand as if turning a key, we took to mean a safe. Brit radioed it back to Smeet who was on coms duty that night. We then noticed Billy's mam get up off the chair and answer the phone. We could see she wasn't happy about something, but we didn't know what at the time. She slammed the phone down and sat back at the table with her head in her hands. Just then Evo and Billy came down dressed to kill on a night out (and probably smelling like a tart's handbag!). Billy's mam got up and headed into the kitchen. She called out to Billy to go in. As he did we could see something was wrong. Brit got on the radio, informing the lads something seemed wrong. Tony and Platty were outside the club and called back to say that Paul had come out of the club with five more men. They'd jumped into two cars and headed off.

There was nothing anyone could do except wait.

Shit had hit the fan. The two cars turned up at Paul's house and all got out. Chris got on the net, "Looking interesting lads," he said. "Looks like the two cars from the club have arrived at the house." Evo was still in the living room with Billy and his mam. Dunc watched as the front door closed behind the last man. All vision was now on me and Brit, and none of us expected what was about to happen.

When the men entered the living room the door closed

behind them. Evo stood up, and Billy went straight to his dad, as if to plead with him. Evo was looking all around him, as if to be looking for a way out. I looked at Brit and he looked straight back at me; we both had the same look of concern on our faces – something was going on that we didn't like. Just as I turned back, I saw Evo running into the kitchen trying to escape – there was nothing we could do.

I got straight on the net, the first thing I had to do was tell Dunc and Chris to sit tight. Smeet came straight back, "Do you need back up?"

"*No no no*, sit tight!"

Brit looked at me with anger in his eyes. Brit, Dunc and Evo had been good friends long before I or Chris had joined the regiment, so I could understand his feelings. "We have to sit tight mate," I said. "We can't let this mission go wrong … if we fail, that's it for us."

Brit understood, but it was hard for him not to help.

Evo had the back door open and was about to run, when a giant of a man grabbed him and smashed his head off the door frame. A shiver ran down my neck, the pain I felt in the pit of my stomach brought back the time my face was smashed into the floor of the van when me, Brit and Kenny were taken. At that moment I wanted to jump the fence and help him.

Brit started to get up, but I held him back, even though it hurt like hell. The look on my face said enough; Brit knew I was right.

By this time Evo was in the garden and three of them had started laying into him. Evo wasn't the biggest of men, but I knew he would retaliate. He managed to pull one of the men to the ground and as he did, he sank his teeth into the right cheek. The man screamed like a baby. Evo couldn't hold on for long, as the others laid into him. It was hell watching, but we knew we had to sit back and let it happen. I felt sick, not because Evo was getting a good kicking, but because I couldn't do anything to help. Me and Evo had become good friends and that made it even harder; I knew from my good hiding, that it wouldn't last long.

What had made them go for Evo?

At first we couldn't work it out, but then the penny dropped. As far as Paul was concerned Evo was down there working and had no family with him. Yes, he had mates with him, but a normal group of lads probably would think he had gone off in a huff for some reason and had just headed home, so he wouldn't be missed. It turned out Billy had been used several times to befriend people to later use them for one thing or another – a hunt, a fight, or just to set up for *"a bit of fun"* as Paul called it. But this time was different. Billy really did like Evo, he got on well with him, and that's what he had been arguing with his dad about.

After the twats had finished giving Evo a kicking they tied him up and put him in the garage. Did we chance going in to check on him, or would it be too risky? Tony and the lads back at the house had to make the decision. We on site would look at Evo as the priority, but unfortunately he wasn't at the moment. What to do next was the question.

Tony and Donny decided to pay Brawdy a visit, and we had to be one hundred per cent sure of the location of the hunt. Smeet got on to BSM Bob for confirmation that we were doing the right thing. It was okayed. BSM Bob would contact Brawdy for Tony and Donny to be met at the gates on their arrival. I knew what was going to happen: Donny would not stop hitting Mal until he got everything out of him, and even then I didn't think he would stop. And I was proved right.

When Tony and Donny entered the guard room they told the sergeant to leave them. Mal was still in pain from the last kicking we had given him, but that wasn't going to stop them ...

I'll not elaborate on what happened next, let's just say they got what they were after – the hunt wasn't going to be at Dartmoor but on the Brecon Beacons.

Why had Mal not informed us before about it?

Christopher McVeigh

(Chris)

Royal Artillery, 1981 to 2004

I suppose it is the same as us, you only give what you have to, never give the enemy more than you need to. At times you can get away with it, but unfortunately for Mal, he didn't on this occasion.

By now me and Brit had been thinking of going into the garage to see how Evo was. Brit got on the net to speak with Smeet about it, but Smeet informed him not to, as Evo's watch had a tracker in it and it was too risky for the team.

After what had previously happened to me, Brit and Kenny, and now Evo, we knew that this type of people didn't care who they got, or where, just as long as they had their fun and had a chance to make money, *big* money.

I was starting to feel really bad for Evo, I knew what he was going to go through, and it wasn't going to be nice, but I understood Smeet's reason to leave him in the garage. What we had to do now, was to make sure that we didn't lose Evo.

The lads had all arrived back at the house and now they had to sort out a plan. Things had changed, and not for the better; it was now against us once again and things had to move fast. Me, Brit, Kenny and Glenn were still in the hides and we had to stay there until things started to happen, which wasn't good for us. We had rations for three days but didn't want to be there that long, but now Evo was in the garage we couldn't take the chance of being seen. This meant we had to stay put.

Kenny was asked to think about what had happened to me, him and Brit, and think of anything we had not mentioned in the past to the lads, something, anything that might help. So Kenny went off to a virtual bedroom to think. It was something he did. I remember in training (we'd hit it off from the start, and we seemed to have worked each other out) the one thing Kenny always did was take himself off, to think about everything that was needed, and he thought he could have the answer to.

Back at the hide, Brit told me to get my head down for an hour or two. Me and Brit had an understanding. Me, him and Evo had been in the same sub unit in the Falklands, so we had got to know each other well, and I think that's what had made this so hard, Brit and me, sitting only feet away from Evo but not being able to do a thing to help him. During our time down in the Falklands we had become very close friends, and we understood each other.

Suddenly there was movement. A Ford transit van had stopped in the street, right outside Paul's house. There were two men in the front. As they got out of the van, Glenn got on the net. Brit hadn't long told me to get my head down, when he gave me a jab in the side to wake me.

"BIG BOB" were the first words that Glenn said. *"Stand by, Stand by"* were the next.

Big Bob was one of the men, the other Glenn had seen at the club but didn't know who he was. The back doors of the van opened, and out got two more men. As they walked down the driveway to the house, the front door opened. Kenny then came on the net; four was the call, four men at the house plus whoever was still in it. As they spoke to Paul one of them headed back to the van and started to reverse it down the drive. Glenn came back on the net, he was contacting Smeet:

"Get ready to move *AND MOVE QUICKLY.*"

The rest of my lads back at the house had all jumped up and grabbed the equipment; they'd loaded up the van and cars. This was it, it had started again, *another hunt*. A shiver ran down my spine, the hairs on my whole body stood up. Brit looked across at me, and I could see he was feeling the same.

At that moment the garage doors opened, and out came Evo bound up. We couldn't see, but Kenny could see it all, and he gave a running commentary of what was happening. Glenn was upset by it all, we had become a family and you felt every blow each other got.

His head was down and he was covered in blood, he wasn't holding himself up. Two of the men seemed to be dragging him along, his hands tied behind his back. A third grabbed his legs, and the three of them just launched him into the van. Glenn's voice changed, you could feel the pain in it. The doors slammed shut and the men started to climb into the van and cars. Paul's car was at the front of the queue. Two of the men came out of the house carrying four backpacks and two cases, and all six got put into the boot of Paul's car. As they drove away up the street, me and Brit got out of the hide, headed down into the park, and up the track to the street, where Glenn and Kenny joined us. There was nothing we could do but sit and wait to be picked up.

The lads had set off and would be with us in about ten minutes. Those ten minutes seemed like a lifetime. We didn't speak, except for a few odd words, *twats! ... fuck the lot of them!* ... and the one everybody says, *if only I ... we ... they ...* but none of it made a difference, we had to go with what we had. Evo was in trouble and we hoped to help him, and to get to the bottom of the reason for the hunts. They could be just *'for fun'*, but we felt there had to be more to this sick game though.

The lads arrived with all three cars and the coms van. Me and Brit jumped into the front car with Donny, Kenny got into the next with Dunc, Platty in the coms van with Smeet and Tony, and finally Jock, Chris and Glenn in the third. Off we set. Smeet was on the tracker watching Evo's movements, it was definitely heading to the Brecons.

When we caught up with the convoy of the dicks we had to act fast. The doormen were big lads and could handle themselves. Smeet gave the instruction for the front car to get in between their last car and us, that was us, keeping back far enough to not alert them (not that they would have suspected anything). We did this. Smeet then got the second car to get in front of my car. Platty was driving, and he did an excellent job. He drove as if the car had been nicked, flying past the doormen's car and me. Glenn hid his face and stuck up his fingers to the doormen – well that's the sort of thing kids do when they nick a car, just to try and get a chase. As Platty got past us, he slowed down, but still kept a short distance between the rest of the doormen.

Then Smeet gave the word for the rest of us to stop the last doorman's car we had between us. The adrenaline was pumping. Although some of us had been in the hides and were a bit worn out, we were still up for it. Jock slowed down, forcing the doormen to do the same. We could see it was getting to them. As their mates were starting to disappear into the distance, all we had to do was wait for them to try and overtake us. Just then a car heading in the opposite direction had his headlights on full beam, and Jock was blinded. Chris grabbed the wheel and whipped it to the left, just in time.

The wings clipped but Chris held it tight and steady away from a full on smash. The other car managed to stay on the road, but he wasn't going to turn back to confront us. It was a dark county road, and he was the one at fault. Just as they got out of sight, Jock made his move.

He slammed the brakes on, forcing the doormen to pull out into the opposite side of the road. As they did, Jock whipped the wheel over and forced them off the road. Their right front wheel hit a ditch, stopping them going anywhere else. We all jumped out of the cars and van. We had to overpower them and do it quickly. Me and Brit grabbed the passengers' doors at the front and rear, as Tony and Smeet grabbed the driver's and offside rear. The men didn't have a clue what was going on. I dragged the first one out, and as he twisted towards me, I brought up my left knee up and smashed it straight to his mouth. I felt his teeth snap, and one stuck into my knee, god it hurt, but the pleasure of getting one of the twats overpowered the pain. By the time I looked up, all four were on the ground, two of them were out cold, the other was screaming out, HELP HELP, but no help was going to come for him, or any of his mates. The feeling of hate came over me and I turned and sank my right foot square in his face. As his nose snapped and his head fell back over to the ground, I felt a sense of pleasure overwhelm me, as if I had just won some competition. Why, I didn't know, I'm not a violent man, but it felt good. Maybe I was getting revenge for the Yorkshire moors, or was it for all the bullying I'd gone through as a kid? I wasn't sure but it felt so good anyway.

We dragged the doormen into the woods at the side of the road. We bound and gagged them, and tied them to a tree until we could get back for them.

This time we had to move them, the SAS wouldn't get involved at this point. We dragged them deep into the woods, found a small clearing, checked the area. The land hadn't been disturbed, so we knew this would be a safe place to leave them. When we got back to the roadside, we checked their car over; it looked OK, just minor body damage. We lifted it back onto the road, and it was OK, so we thought if we took it with us, we may get closer to the rest of them if needed. Glenn jumped in the driver's seat, and I got in beside him. We set off down the road with the rest of the lads.

We knew Platty was about five to six miles ahead of us, so we put our foot down, to make up ground.

Platty was OK. The rest of the doormen in the cars would think it was their mates behind them anyway. We managed to catch up after about fifteen minutes. The plan now was to do the same again, this would give us the advantage, take them out one car at a time. We hadn't planned for this but we couldn't let Evo go through what me, Brit and Kenny had been through. We got into position ready to move. Platty would be the front car again as it had worked last time (and if something works you don't change it) except this time it *didn't* work out. As he started to move, the car he was about to overtake pulled out, as if to stop the overtake. The car in front thought it was his mate, so he decided to have a bit of fun by stopping him getting past. Smeet got on the net, instructing Platty to pull out of the overtake – we had to think of something else and quick.

Smeet had jumped into the back of the van as it was heading down the road. He opened one of the drawers on the coms desk, pulled out a map and started to study it. He came over the net: "About one mile down the road is a left turn, that is the last one for about ten miles." It was more a track than a road, but he reckoned it would be quicker and it would bring us back onto the road ahead of them. We left Platty's car to follow them just in case there was another track they could go down and we lost them. We could keep track on him anyway as all the cars we had had been fitted with trackers. Smeet reckoned we should end up about four minutes ahead of them when we hit the main road again.

The track was rough going, but that wasn't an issue for us, we had driven in rougher terrain than this. As we drove we all were thinking of what to do next, then Chris came on the air: *"SMASH ONE OF THEM OFF THE ROAD"*. We didn't understand what he meant, so Tony asked him to clarify.

"Once we hit the junction to the main road, we deploy ourselves along the road and wait for the doormen's cars to arrive. Glenn and Geordie are in one of their cars, let the front cars and van get past the junction, then Glenn pulls out of the junction, smashing them off the road, and we'll be waiting to jump them. Patty can get past and continue on their tail."

We all thought about it, and that was it – we couldn't come up with anything else. When we arrived at the junction we had 4½ minutes to get into position, all the cars and van had been parked out of sight of the main road. Glenn informed me to get out and help them – *"it only takes one to drive this heap* – and if Glenn had his mind on doing it, I wasn't going to stop him (not that he would have listened anyway).

As I was getting out Glenn unplugged his earpiece and switched up the volume, at times it was better not to have an earpiece in. He put the car into position and waited for the words, Go Go Go. As I ran to the junction to join the rest of the lads, Jock was giving out the instruction. (Well, it was his idea so we let him get on with it. We all knew he was capable of heading the task – as were we all – I think that's how we all got on so well.)

Three of us lined the road, with about 50 yards apart. As the car would pass we would call out *one* the man, *two* the second, and *three* the third; Glenn would count it down *1, 2, 3,* then 4. He would move on 3 and the timing would be spot on to hit the car just right. The rest of the lads would be sitting in ambush on the side of the road, in a hidden and safe area. Once the cars hit, we had to wait for Platty to pass, then make our move.

It couldn't have worked any better if we had practised it for days. Spot on. Glenn got the timing just right, this time the car flew off the road and into some woods on the right side of the road. As we waited, Kenny and Dunc had their arms out of the windows waving like mad (nice one lads!) as they flew past. Platty was concentrating on not hitting Glenn's car. It worked and we couldn't have been happier, straight in we went, four men in the car (that was a big help, the more we took out then the better advantage we would have later) two of them were out cold, or so we thought at first, but one of them was dead. Not one of us felt sorry for him. It was as if we were back in the Falklands, and the aim was to take them out *no matter what.*

The other two had been in the back, no seatbelts on and I think that was what killed the one in the front, a head to the back of the head of his mate.

Once we got them out of the car and had tied them up, the hard part was then moving the car. We had to push it further into the woods and cover it up. Once all that was done off we set. Once again Smeet sent a coms message to BSM Bob back at camp. Now we had to catch up with Platty, and work out what we had to do next.

Now there was only one car and a van to deal with. At the most we thought five or six men, and there were eleven of us, so we could now think about stopping them together.

As we hit the road again Dunc got on the radio to inform us the doormen had pulled into a car park. There was one more car there, its occupants appeared to be waiting to meet someone. Whether they were there to meet with the doormen or not we didn't know at this time, we would have to get closer to find out.

Platty carried on driving. That was when the doormen would realise it hadn't been their mates behind them. As Platty drove past the parking area, they started to descend down a hill. At the same time the road started to wind off to the right. They drove a further 400 yards or so when they came to a track. Platty stopped the car and Dunc got out to check the area, to see if they could hide the car. They could then head back to the parking area on foot.

Kenny got on the net to inform the rest of us what they intended to do. I gave the command for all headlights to be switched off, and to free-wheel. There were no street lights, and no road markings to keep us on the road, but this was something we had done many times before, so it wasn't a problem to any of us. As we slowed down, myself and Glenn jumped out and ran ahead of the cars, to listen out for anything we could hear – a car engine or chatting among the doormen. It didn't take long. The headlights still on and the men laughing and chatting among themselves. Now we had to hide the cars, but it wasn't going to be so easy. There were no tracks; there was just a small lay-by that was just long enough to hold all the cars and the van. We took out all the equipment we would need and headed off on foot.

As we got close to the parking area, we split up. Around the parking area was a stone wall. There were three gaps in the wall, two for footpaths leading off into the moors, and the other was the car entrance and exit. Each group of us had a radio and had to relay back to Tony and Smeet anything we saw, just so we all knew what was going on around us. Platty, Dunc and Kenny had got in position ahead of us so they were the first to relay back: there were nine men altogether, two of which had been in the car that had been in the parking area before the doormen, and seven from the doormen we had been following. Two of the men kept looking out of the parking area, presumably looking for their mates that we had already taken out. I was with Glenn and Chris. I noticed one of the men go into the boot of the car that had already been in the parking area, and take out a case, and it looked heavy by the way he was carrying it. As he was doing that, two of the doormen did the same from one of their cars. They then laid the cases down in front of Paul and one of the men they had met there. Both men bent down and opened the cases at the same time. They both then checked the contents of each other's case. What was in them we couldn't see, but it had to be something important. They both then stood up and shook hands, they swapped cases and put them in the cars, and headed to the van where Evo was. As they opened the back doors, I held my breath. Was Evo going to get another good hiding, as they'd done with me before they let me, Brit and Kenny run off into the Yorkshire moors?

We couldn't see the state Evo was in, but it was clear he wasn't in a good way, by the way he was being dragged along the ground. What the hell was happening? Evo had been bundled into the boot of the car of the two men that the doormen had just met. *SHIT!* This looked as if it was a *sale*. Had they just *paid* the doormen for Evo as part of a transaction? We couldn't let this happen, we *had* to put a stop to this as soon as we could.

I got on to the radio and made a suggestion to Smeet. *DO IT* was the reply. I ran back to the car as fast as I could. As I did the rest of the lads got into position. With everyone at the ready, I got to the car and contacted Smeet again: *READY TO ROLL READY TO ROLL*. As I waited for go, I heard each one of the groups come back, *IN POSITION IN POSITION*, then it came, *START YOUR ENGINE*.

As I sat with my engine running, I could feel the adrenaline pumping through my body; my hands became sweaty and my throat dry, but I was ready for this, I had waited a long time to get my revenge, and I wasn't going to waste this opportunity. Then it came *GO GO GO*. I dipped the clutch, pushed the gear stick into first, switched on the headlights, and took off as fast as I could. Up into second, then third, I was now hitting 45mph, the engine was screaming and I hit it up into fourth, 55mph and I could see the headlights of the cars in the parking area, the men all seemed to jump up as if to say *what the hell is this?*

I headed straight towards the entrance, ripped on the handbrake and in a split second the car swung side on to the entrance, stopping dead in the centre of the entrance. As it did the headlights of the doormen's cars went out. Kenny, Jock, Chris and Brit had jumped over the walls and headed straight for the cars putting the lights out. As they did, Tony Glenn, Smeet, Donny and Platty headed for the doormen and their two new mates. We all had weapons, clubs and the like. My job was now to head for the car with Evo in. Dunc had also been instructed to do the same.

As we opened it, a small light came on and we could see Evo looking back at us. My eyes filled up and so did Dunc's, the pain in Evo's face was hell. All I could say was sorry, but it wouldn't fix him. I felt it was all my doing, if only I had got to Brit and Kenny sooner at that nightclub in Lincolnshire all them months ago none of this would have happened... but feeling sorry for myself wouldn't get us out of this one, so I gave myself a shake, and grabbed Evo with Dunc, put him over the wall and headed in to help the lads. I got my eye on one jumping the wall and heading down the road. Tony was on his tail, so I left him to it, and headed in to give the rest of the lads a hand. With us being in the dark for a while, our eyes had adapted to the dark a lot quicker. The doormen didn't have a clue what was going on. Glenn headed for Paul and smashed him in the side of the head with a truncheon he had brought with him. Paul hit the ground like a sack of spuds.

Brit and Kenny knocked one out cold, with what seemed to be 100 punches, the speed of them was unreal. One of the doormen tried to jump in a car to head off, but unluckily for him, Smeet had run at the car, jumped up with two feet smashing against the door, jamming the lad's arm in it. Smeet then jumped up off the ground, dragged the lad out of the car, smashing him to the ground. He ripped his arms behind his back and then tied them up. The lad's arms were clearly broken. Once Smeet had tied his hands, he swung him over onto his back and smashed him in the face, knocking him out cold. By this time it was all over. Bodies lay strewn around, bloody and broken.

We started to gather them together and I noticed one missing – we had forgotten about Big Bob, *WHERE THE HELL WAS HE?* Me, Kenny and Brit headed out of the car park onto the road. Nothing. But just then I noticed a silhouette on the top of a hill to my left. That had to be him. We couldn't let him get away, he was the one I wanted the most. What he had done to me back on the moors, he wasn't going to get away with it. And Kenny was behind me. I kept looking up so as not to lose him. Then I noticed two more silhouettes up ahead, but this time I knew who they were. Donny and Glenn. They had spotted him before we had and had a good headstart on us.

As I climbed higher up the hill, I could hear screaming from over the hill. Donny and Glenn had got to him, and by the sounds of it, they weren't shaking his hand. By the time I got to them, Big Bob's hands had been tied behind his back and he was being marched back to the car park. I could hear him begging Glenn and Donny to let him go and he would tell them anything they needed to know. Just then something flashed past me. It was Kenny and Brit – nothing was going to stop them getting to him. The two of them jumped straight onto him, and then the screams started again. Donny and Glenn stood back; they knew what we had been through and felt we should at least give him a good kicking. As they did I grabbed them and pulled them off him. The two of them turned to set about me. *"WHAT THE HELL ARE YOU DOING?"* Brit yelled as he grabbed me by the throat.

"We need him to speak, he has to know the most and we need information? Handing Evo over to that bloke, there has to be something else going on, and *he* has to know what, ... *DON'T YOU?"* And I turned to Bob and smashed my head into his face. Down he went like a big lump, crying like a little baby. The lads new what I meant, but couldn't work out why I had stuck one on him. (Well, I wasn't going to let them have all the fun!)

We headed back to the car park and put him with the rest. The lads had Paul to one side, Chris and Jock were slapping him in the face, but he wasn't going to speak with just slaps. I dragged him over to the back of one of the cars, while Platty and Smeet dragged Bob over and sat him down in front of Paul. We started to tell Paul how we had found him and his mates, all thanks to Bob. Bob wasn't liking this at all. I also informed Paul about Bob killing one of his own so he could have the money to himself, then I bent Paul forward, cut the rope that held his hands behind his back, and did the same to Bob. Bob was begging us to keep Paul off him. Paul, we could see, wouldn't have that. Although he was a bad one, he was like us, never turn on your own.

We let Paul give him a bit of a kicking, then we pulled him off and tied him up again, took him to the van, put them all in, and headed back to Bob. In the meantime Evo had been looked after by Tony. He was in a bad way but he'd be fine was the call. Chris and Dunc had opened the cases and we couldn't believe it ... Paul's case was full of cash, and the other contained small packets of a white powder. What it was we didn't know, but we all could guess. This was not something we could deal with, so Smeet got on the net and BSM Bob arranged for the pickup of them all. The SAS was now taking over this job; we couldn't go any further with this, it was way out of our league.

It turned out to be a very big international gang and Big Bob as we called him, was not big at all. It turned out he squealed like a little pig, and gave the SAS everything they needed – for a deal that would keep him out of harm's reach. As for us, we headed back to camp and got on with the jobs we had signed up for, what an everyday soldier was paid to do – clean Land Rovers, repair com nets … and guard duties.

Or so we all thought.

Also by John Gordon

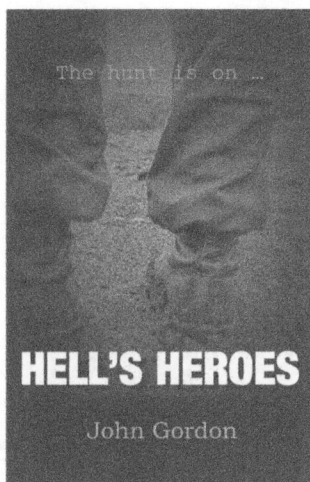

Hell's Heroes

Available now

ISBN: 978-1-78222-827-1

"At the beginning we were all sworn to secrecy; this was never to be spoken about outside of the group. After 35 years I feel I can now tell my story as it happened."

A veteran's tale: exhilarating, heart-breaking and loyal to the cause.